Free to Love: the Cinema of the Sexual Revolution

Free to Love: the Cinema of the Sexual Revolution

International House Philadelphia

Contents

Contents

Jesse Pires

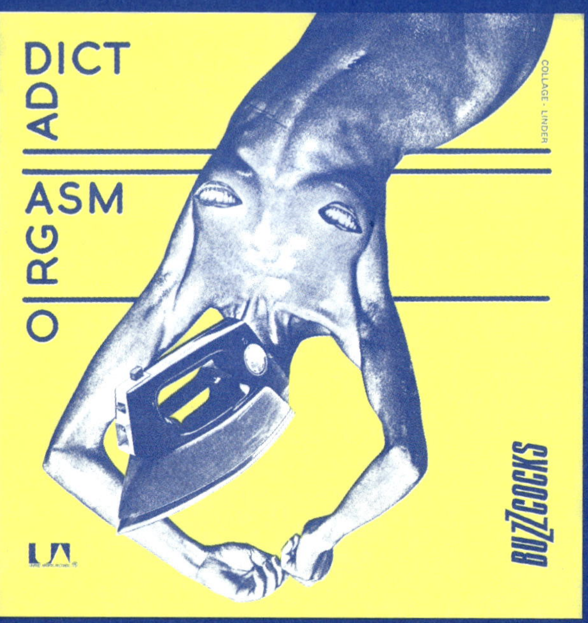

Buzzcocks, *Orgasm Addict*, 1977
Artwork by Linder

Introduction:
Free to Love

A few years ago I was watching Hal Ashby's excellent 1974 film *Shampoo*, and I was struck by how aptly it captured an important turning point in American culture. The story of a charismatic hair stylist played by Warren Beatty and his numerous sexual relationships, the film is set in 1968 amid what we now regard as the high-water mark of liberalism, and it both symbolically and literally foreshadows the ultimate undoing of the New Left in the wake of Nixon's election to the US presidency.

Beatty's George Roundy defies the traditional values of the 1950s, yet he ultimately demonstrates the limits of the sexual revolution's utopian aspirations. By sleeping around Hollywood—and it's no accident that Ashby's film takes place inside a bastion of commercial art, where promiscuity is practically an ethos—he literally screws himself out of power, and his self-betrayal is transcribed onto the failures of 1960s countercultures to truly make a difference in society. Of course, we know the rest of the story: the longing for order and safety brought on by Nixon, then the even more reactionary Reagan, who rang in "morning in America"—namely, the morning after those tumultuous, revolutionary days of sexual liberation and youth rebellion. As a time capsule of a time capsule (the film, just six years after the fact, is already looking back on a lost era), *Shampoo* interrogates the legacy of the sexual revolution, a cultural coitus interruptus. And those questions, in a sense, are what inspired "Free to Love."

While it's difficult to articulate every aspect of the sexual revolution in a single film series, we attempted to cover a broad panoply of visions from the era with the hope that they might begin to demonstrate just how entangled sexual liberation and popular entertainment became and how much our society has changed in the decades since.

"Free to Love" brings together a wide selection of films, both commercial and experimental, to investigate how these issues and ideas manifested themselves in the production of moving-image art. Some of these films have experienced an enduring popularity over the years while others have rarely been screened since their initial release. The sexual revolution, as defined by this film series, begins in the early 1960s and ends in the late 1970s. It encompasses the publication of Helen Gurley Brown's *Sex and the Single Girl*, the mass availability of oral contraception, the Stonewall riots, and, of course, the sudden rise in popularity of erotic cinema. While the sexual revolution cannot simply be viewed as a single unified movement, it is precisely its very conflicts and contradictions that inspired some of the most important films from this period, asserting sexual power in an era when "power to the people" was the motto.

It turns out that film conveyed this revolution perfectly, bringing it to the most polite corners of conversation. Today, it's hard to imagine middle-class, suburban couples lining up to attend a screening of a pornographic film, but for a brief moment that was de rigueur. Gerard Damiano's film *Deep Throat* was screened in seventy-three US cities and made $25 million in ticket sales.[1]

In and of itself, sex on film was nothing new. Dudley Murphy's 1921 short film *Soul of the Cypress* is a haunting erotic fantasy featuring full-frontal nudity. There's even a cut to exploding fireworks as the main characters presumably reach sexual climax (a device later used in numerous films including *Deep Throat*).[2] It was simply that, over the years, the audience had changed.

In the postwar years the films, performances, and happenings of artists like Jack Smith, Carolee Schneemann, and Claes Oldenburg often involved sexually explicit or transgressive elements, so that one can begin to see the seeds of the mainstream erotic cinema being sown in the lofts and galleries of urban bohemia. It also didn't hurt that Smith's *Flaming Creatures*, a forty-five minute film where male and female bodies writhe in a whimsical display of Dionysian delight, made headline news as it was deemed obscene by the authorities and consistently confiscated by local police departments at various screenings across the country.[3]

In the age of the internet, these images are perhaps no longer all that groundbreaking and some may even seem quaint by current standards. But the questions they pose continue to be provocative, or at the very least relevant. In 2013, we're still talking about a "war on women," so we know that sexual power remains a critical and pressing issue. For all of its liberations, the sexual revolution also brought on a long-running backlash that has relegated erotic content to the smallest and most private screens. Gone are the days of standing in line for an X-rated film— now, everyone stars in their own.

In the end I decided not to include *Shampoo* in the series even though its influence may be felt throughout the entire program. There are, undoubtedly, other omissions, including several films that have all but vanished from circulation. Nevertheless, this series is surely the most ambitious attempt to capture the narrative of the sexual revolution on film to date. I hope that "Free to Love" will provide a fresh perspective on the changes that took place, not just in cinema but in politics, academia, and the arts and, most importantly, on individuals who dramatically threw off the shackles of a fearful, hypocritical, and antiquated system of moral authority and suppression to live their lives any way they chose. A culture that can acknowledge and appreciate sex as a natural and healthy activity that unites us all and allows each of us to connect with our innermost passions is most certainly a place beyond fear, repression, and ignorance. "Free to Love" is perhaps a small, albeit partial glimpse of such a place.

1.
David Allyn, *Make Love, Not War. The Sexual Revolution: An Unfettered History* (Boston: Little, Brown, 2000), 234.

2.
David E. James, *The Most Typical Avant-Garde* (Berkeley, CA: University of California Press, 2005), 27.

3.
Scott MacDonald, *Canyon Cinema, The Life and Times of an Independent Film Distributor* (Berkeley, CA: University of California Press, 2008), 47.

International House Philadelphia and I are grateful for the contributions and assistance of the following people; A.K. Burns, Michael Chaiken, Jon Gartenberg, Elena Gorfinkel, Ed Halter, Barbara Hammer, J. Hoberman, Alex Klein, Andrew Lampert, Radley Metzger, Peter Nesbett, Pat Rocco, Eric Schaefer, M.M. Serra, A.L. Steiner, Jack Stevenson, Whitney Strub, Drake Stutesman and Todd Weiner of the UCLA Film & Television Archive. In addition I would like to acknowledge the guidance and expertise of Sheryl Conkelton, Joseph N. Newland, Mark Owens, and Greenhouse Media. Special thanks to Elisa Ludwig for her encouragement. This project would not be possible without the generosity and support of the Pew Center for Arts and Heritage.

J. Hoberman

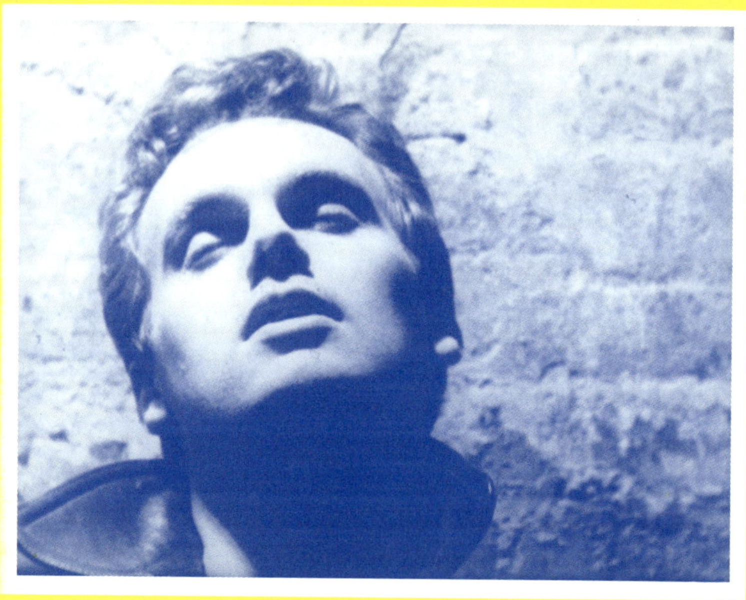

Andy Warhol, *Blow Job*, 1964

Freed to Love? Movies and Sexual Revolution

In the 1920s, movies themselves were the sexual revolution. Motion pictures were the fantasy machine par excellence. As avant-garde filmmaker Kenneth Anger wrote of those who were movie stars in his ecstatically scurrilous *Hollywood Babylon*, "Never have so few…furnished masturbation fodder for so many." In the 1960s and 1970s when, thanks to the availability of 16mm and the collapse of the Motion Picture Association of America Code, the dream machine was hijacked, the movies were enlisted—not only to embody but to represent.[1]

Anger's 1947 *Fireworks*, a brash and poetic homoerotic psychodrama produced by the teenaged artist in his family living room while his parents were away for a few days, was a harbinger of things to come. Sixteen years later, the film-maker Gregory Markopoulos would report that the first viewers of Jack Smith's pansexual, polymorphously perverse *Flaming Creatures* (1963)—a virtual home movie, shot on outdated film stock and staged on a Lower East Side roof-top—"were projected into a state of cosmic or filmic shock."

There had never been anything quite like Smith's com-bination of casual nudity, childlike dress-up, and desultory (or occasionally manic) sex play. For Markopoulos it was as though the 30-year-old sometime photographer liberated the cinema's unconscious. "Those images, scenes and sequences which [*Flaming Creatures*' original audience] had envisioned and had wished would appear in the commercial film which they attended were unexpectedly offered before their eyes.... The audience burst forth and roared, while the walls of cen-sorship began to crack."

Crack but not yet collapse. Embraced by the under-ground, the movie Smith described as "a comedy set in a haunted movie studio" was deemed pornographic; prints were confiscated in New York City and elsewhere, there was a trial, and *Flaming Creatures* became a *cause célèbre* that would ultimately figure in the 1968 confirmation of a Supreme Court chief justice. Nevertheless, Smith lit a fire. Barbara Rubin was not yet twenty when she made her far more graphic amateur orgy *Christmas on Earth* (1964); Andy Warhol's bluntly titled *Blow Job* (1964) was an exercise in conceptual pornography, consisting solely of a man's face in ecstatic close-up as he was presumably fellated by an off-screen partner.

Artists also made more personal statements, most spectacularly Carolee Schneemann, whose 1967 *Fuses* was something like a sexual psychodrama—documenting the film-maker and her lover James Tenney in the throes of physical passion. Anything but clinical (Schneemann would compare the camera's gaze to that of her pet cat), *Fuses* was further naturalized over the course of the several years that the artist spend subjecting her footage to heat, rain, and wind. Subsequent sexually explicit portraits (by Scott Bartlett, Stan Brakhage, Barbara Hammer, and others) were more romantic; other treatments of human intimacy, notably *Schmeerguntz* (1965) by Gunvor Nelson and Dorothy Wiley, were relent-lessly demystifying.

In any case, by the late sixties eros was the subject that defined American avant-garde cinema. San Francisco filmmaker James Broughton's lyrically wholesome, program-matically democratic sex celebration *The Bed* was the short film hit of the 1968 New York Film Festival. (A year later, the NYFF's opening-night movie would be Hollywood's send-up of the sexual revolution, *Bob & Carol & Ted & Alice*.) Meanwhile underground movies with even fleeting glimpse of nudity were shown in Times Square theaters. The first "beaver" films to be theatrically exhibited in New York were advertised with the declaration: "Underground!! So…You Think You've Seen Everything!!!" Warhol and his assistant Paul Morrissey were already merging underground and sexploitation with movies like *Bike Boy, Nude Restaurant,*

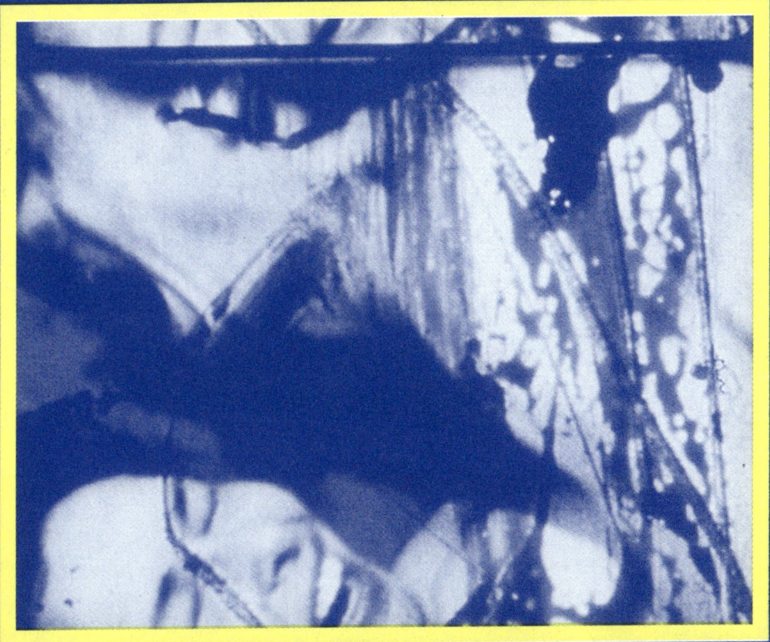

Carolee Schneemann, *Fuses*, 1967

Freed to Love

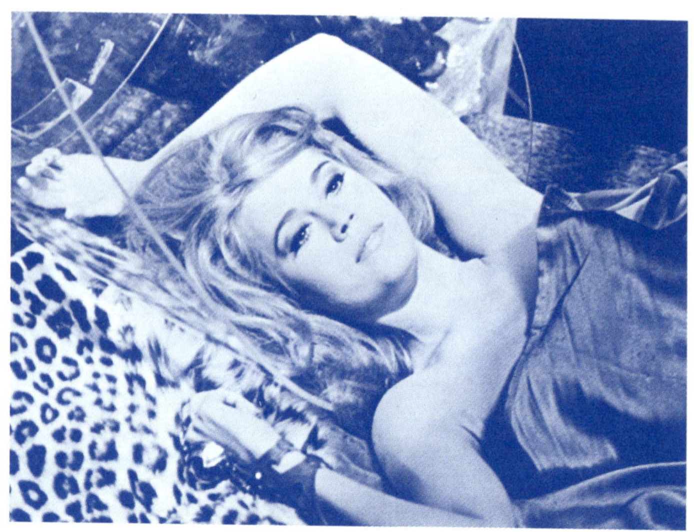

Roger Vadim, *Barbarella*, 1968

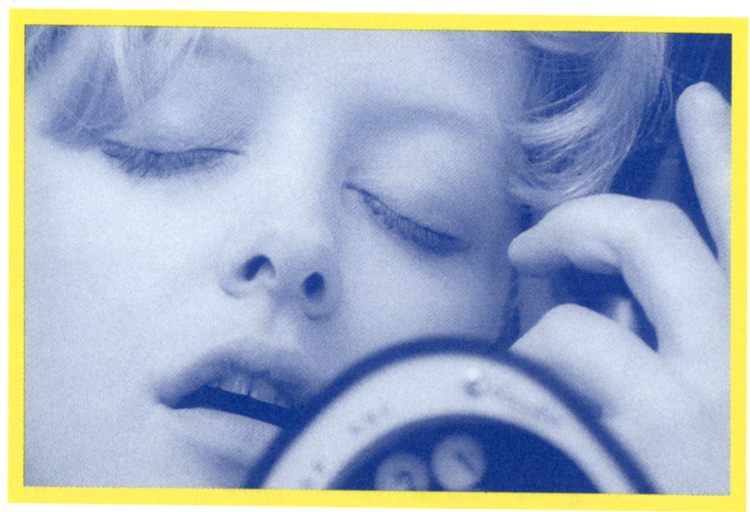

Nelson Lyon, *The Telephone Book*, 1971

and *I, A Man* (originally conceived as a vehicle for rock Dionysus Jim Morrison) (all 1967).[2]

The commercialization of the cinematic sexual revolution was already underway when, in August 1967, midway through the so-called Summer of Love, *I, A Man* opened off Times Square, with its title an homage to a then-notorious and extremely successful Swedish release, *I, A Woman* (1965). Between 1967 and 1970, American skin-flick auteurs like Russ Meyer, the nudie-cutie Cecil DeMille, and the more Euro-artistic Radley Metzger—who distributed *I, a Woman* in the US—competed for attention with Scandinavian imports like Knud Leif Thomsen's *Gift* (aka *Venom*, 1966), Annelise Meineche's *Without a Stitch* (1968), and Vilgot Sjöman's *I Am Curious (Yellow)* (1967), all of which appeared here in 1968, although *I Am Curious (Yellow)* required a trial—complete with testimony by Norman Mailer and several well-known film critics—and an appeal to a federal court before its distributor, Grove Press (publisher of *Naked Lunch* and *Tropic of Cancer*), was able to release the movie in March 1969.

In the interim there was French director Roger Vadim's science-fiction comic-strip adaptation *Barbarella* (1968) which, at once coy and graphic, managed to dramatize (if not exploit) Jane Fonda's sexual awakening without recourse to fully unveiling her body. The opening striptease, with Fonda floating weightless in her space capsule, introduced the star as a sex object; far more significant however was the lengthy scene in which, hooked up to some sort of futuristic stimulation device, she achieves orgasm without sexual intercourse. (Not only is Fonda's response shown in close-up but its power and duration short circuits the machine.)

The Telephone Book (1971), an upscale post-underground feature by Warhol's friend the photographer-writer Nelson Lyon, treated the skin-flick phenomenon as a new form of Pop art—even as it adopted the mode's dominant

Freed to Love

narrative template. Sarah Kennedy appeared as a sort of frequently naked Kewpie Doll innocent (not unlike Fonda's Barbarella or Playboy's Little Annie Fanny) undertaking a voyage of sexual discovery amid a galaxy of madcaps and grotesques including the Factory superstar Ultra Violet and the young Jill Clayburgh.

Other post-underground movies were less frivolous in expressing their makers' sexuality. These include the poet Charles Henri Ford's 1971 *Johnny Minotaur*—which took a romantic, openly voyeuristic pleasure in observing good-looking hippie boys making out on the beach in Crete—and photographer James Bidgood's initially anonymous *Pink Narcissus*. Filmed in the artist's living room beginning in the early sixties, and blown up from 8mm to 35mm for its 1971 release, Bidgood's labor of love was a reverie of a sensitive hustler that evoked both *Fireworks* and *Flaming Creatures*, albeit without the taboo-breaking irony that characterized those pioneering films.

The breakthrough in graphic gay sex came at the end of 1971 with the release of Wakefield Poole's *Boys in the Sand*—an episodic series of sexual encounters between con-senting hunks, shot in five days (rather than ten years) on Fire Island, that by some accounts grossed fifty times its $8,000 cost. Poole also had a Warhol connection, having previously made a ten-minute documentary on the artist, but better than Warhol, he understood the meaning of "money shot."

When *I Am Curious (Yellow)* finally opened at the Cinema Rendezvous, near Carnegie Hall in midtown Manhattan, in March 1969, it broke all records for an art film by taking in nearly $80,000 during its first seven days, and would be the first foreign-language film ever to top *Variety's* weekly chart.

Despite using the trope of a young woman's erotic awakening, the movie was hardly an exploitation film—*I Am Curious (Yellow)* and its "sequel" *I Am Curious (Blue)* (1967) were far closer in its method and aspiration to Godardian analysis than to skin-flick prurience. Writer-director Vilgot Sjöman linked his protagonist Lena's sexual curiosity to the questions she raised about Sweden's supposedly classless, democratic, non-militarist society. The movie's most notorious scenes were the comic episodes in which Lena and her boyfriend make love in public, but there was also a far more explicit and discomfiting sequence in which she is treated for the scabies with which her lover presumably infected her.

"That movie was so sick I wasn't even aroused," one senator complained of *Flaming Creatures* when it was screened for members of Congress in 1968. The same logic might explain the hostility directed at Sjöman's notably sober, naturalistic, politically minded, and somewhat lumbering representation of female desire. "The Trash Explosion is here, and *I Am Curious (Yellow)* is at the bottom of the garbage dump," Rex Reed wrote in a *New York Times* piece apparently designed to answer the favorable review given the movie by the newspaper's regular critic Vincent Canby. "This genuinely vile and disgusting Swedish meatball is pseudo-pornography at its ugliest and least titillating."

I Am Curious (Yellow) was certainly of its moment. The early seventies were the moment of Dionysian cults, unisex, dope, and armed love. As proposed by Berkeley activist Jerry Rubin in his 1970 manifesto *Do It!*, "Riots, campus struggles, demonstrations—the longer, the better—are social, community orgies." The movement proposed sex as a weapon. To get naked in public was a moral act.

Sjöman was not the only filmmaker to essay an overtly political sex film. *Bob & Carol & Ted & Alice* (1969), directed by Paul Mazursky from a script he wrote with Larry

Freed to Love

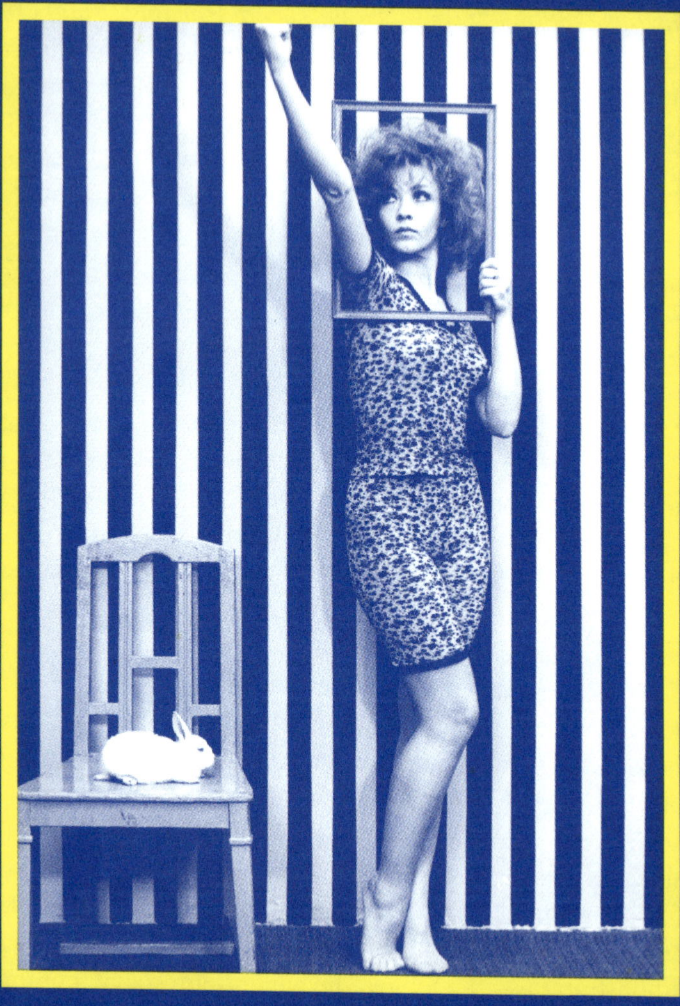

Dušan Makavejev,
WR: Mysteries of the Organism, 1971
Image courtesy of Janus Films

Tucker, not only burlesqued the embourgeoisement of the sexual revolution but also the essentially apolitical new age ideology of self-fulfillment that, not least in the movie industry, attached itself to the new mores. The comedy of a liberated couple (Robert Culp and Natalie Wood, the latter of whom had, a decade before, played a teenage sexual martyr in *Splendor in the Grass,* and then five years later, appeared in the suggestively coy comedy *Sex and the Single Girl*, always in costume) and their attempt to convert their more conventional friends (Elliott Gould and Dyan Cannon), *B&C&T&A* is a feast of embarrassing encounter sessions, sanctimonious cuddle-puddles, and hippie self-righteousness that winds up in Las Vegas—epicenter of the old licentiousness. "First we'll have an orgy and then we'll go see Tony Bennett!" Gould exclaims.[3]

Other movies served as more complex sexual-revolution autocritiques. The sensation of 1971 Cannes Film Festival, Dušan Makavejev's *WR: Mysteries of the Organism*, had its origins in a Ford Foundation grant the Yugoslav filmmaker received to visit the US and research the life of Freud's most radical disciple, Wilhelm Reich. In addition to interviewing Reich's American followers and documenting various types of Reichian therapy, Makavejev shot consider-able travelogue footage among the hippies, drag queens, and sexual activists of New York's East Village.

The most Godardian movie made by anyone other than Jean-Luc Godard, *WR* combines Makavejev's research with a fictional story mocking Communist intellectuals, Yugoslav workers, the Stalin cult, the sacred symbols of World War II partisans, and, above all, Communist puritanism. *WR* was attacked by both orthodox Reichians and orthodox Communists; it was banned in Yugoslavia until 1986 and Makavejev was even threatened with a jail sentence.

Also abrasive, Rosa von Praunheim's *It is Not the Homosexual Who is Perverse, But the Society in Which He*

Freed to Love

Lives was commissioned by West German TV in 1971 but withheld from broadcast by liberal bureaucrats fearful that, shown in the wake of Germany's recent decriminalization of homosexual activity, Prauheim's movie might contribute to a homophobic backlash. Praunheim argued that it was the homosexual who most directly rebelled against the submission of sex to procreation (and the institutions that guarantee the social order). After the telecast however, it was the gay community that was enraged by Praunheim's criticism of bourgeois homosexuality.[4]

The year of *B&C&T&A* a presidential task force on obscenity reported that the new pornography "strongly [paralleled] the rise of certain extremist groups of nihilists." But, as the movie predicted, middle America was enjoying its own porn pandemic. By 1972, there was a startling proliferation of skin flicks, massage parlors, swingers clubs, live sex shows. *The Joy of Sex* was a bestseller; Woody Allen released his parody of another best-selling book, *Everything You Always Wanted to Know About Sex * But Were Afraid to Ask*. The same year brought the first X-rated animated feature, Ralph Bakshi's *Fritz the Cat*, adapted from the underground comic by R. Crumb, and (following in the wake of *Boys in the Sand*) the first crossover hardcore features, *Deep Throat*, *Behind the Green Door*, and *The Devil in Miss Jones*.

Deep Throat, in particular, was a media event and a show business landmark. Shot in a Miami motel for $22,000, it would eventually gross $600 million. Nothing if not high-concept (the premise posits a woman whose clitoris is somewhere near her tonsils seeking sexual gratification through copious oral sex), *Deep Throat* was created by Gerard Damiano, an erstwhile beautician, as a vehicle for the frizzy-haired hippie goddess Linda Lovelace, pimped by her husband for her extraordinary ability to suppress her gag response. *Deep Throat* was the first hardcore porn film to draw dating couples and groups of women. Some, including Damiano, dreamed that the next step would be a Hollywood-porn merger with actual movie stars having real sex on the screen.

That never happened. Rather, *Deep Throat* took the quintessential skin-flick narrative as far as it would go, although, driven by the spectacle of a supposedly free and unfettered female desire, the movie was less bawdy joke than remarkable displacement. *Deep Throat* evoked, even as it concealed, the source of female satisfaction while privileging that satisfaction in the service of a phallocratic regime. (No wonder even libertarian feminists were appalled.) At the same time, with its good-natured humor and (relatively) liberal tolerance of sexual diversity—or at least do-your-thing-ism— *Deep Throat* made light of the porn pandemic that preoccupied much of the nation.[5]

President Nixon had declared war on porn. But what goes around comes around: the source who helped Woodward and Bernstein nail the president to his Watergate cross was named for the movie that, according to *Screw* magazine publisher Al Goldstein, featured "the greatest on-screen fellatio since the birth of Christ."

Be that as it may, *Deep Throat* can be considered the first 1970s blockbuster, anticipating by three summers a movie that began by securing audience complicity with a bloody sex crime, namely *Jaws*. Everyone knew about *Deep Throat*; everyone (who was anyone) had to see it. It was a phenomenon that fed on its own notoriety. Johnny Carson joked about it on TV, the movie was analyzed in the *New York Review of Books,* and declared "porno chic" by the *New York Times.* Early reporting on the film was rife with celebrity sightings. Hardcore had arrived. The revolution was over.

Freed to Love

Thereafter, the major provocations would be international art movies. *Deep Throat* was not yet four months into its run when Bernardo Bertolucci's *Last Tango in Paris*, an X-rated feature spun from the stuff of stag films with the bona fide star Marlon Brando, had its world premiere on the closing night of the 1972 New York Film Festival—a date, wrote Pauline Kael, that "should become a landmark in movie history comparable to May 29, 1913—the night *Le Sacre du Printemps* was first performed."

Kael called *Last Tango* "the most powerfully erotic movie ever made" and "perhaps even the most liberating." Certainly it was the last European art film to engage American cine-mores. Two years later there was Makavejev's *Sweet Movie*, the scandal of the 1974 Cannes Film Festival, which, among other gross attractions, featured the orgiastic antics of Otto Muehl and the Therapie-Kommune of Vienna. Two years after that came Pier Paolo Pasolini's even more scatological, posthumously-released *Salò, or the 120 Days of Sodom*. Finally, there was the sensation of the 1976 Cannes Film Festival, albeit shown not in competition but in the Directors' Fortnight, Nagisa Oshima's *In the Realm of the Senses*.

Like *I Am Curious (Yellow)* eight years earlier, Oshima's movie was seized by US customs, but not before a press screening at the NYFF. ("Some of the persons viewing yesterday's screening said they did not think *In the Realm of the Senses* was any more pornographic than some of the American motion pictures being shown in Times Square houses," the *New York Times* reported.)

Taken with the idea of western pornography but reverting to the traditions of seventeenth- and eighteenth-century Japanese *shunga* woodcuts, Oshima orchestrated a tale of all-consuming passion, based on a true story and sensational crime from the 1930s. (The original Japanese title could be translated as "Bullfight of Love;" the English title is derived

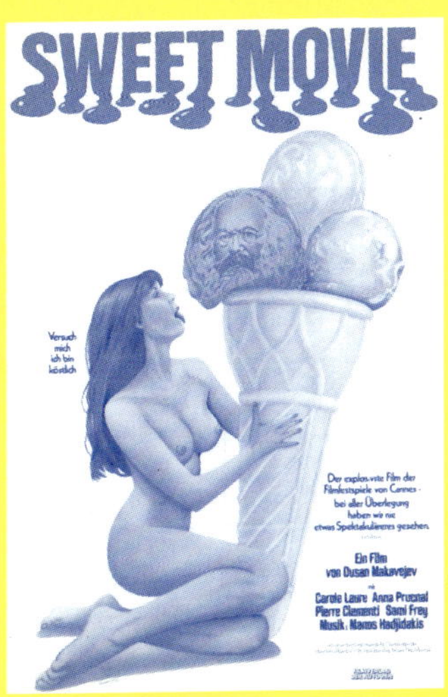

Logo for Bernardo Bertolucci,
Last Tango in Paris, 1972

Dušan Makavejev,
Sweet Movie, 1974

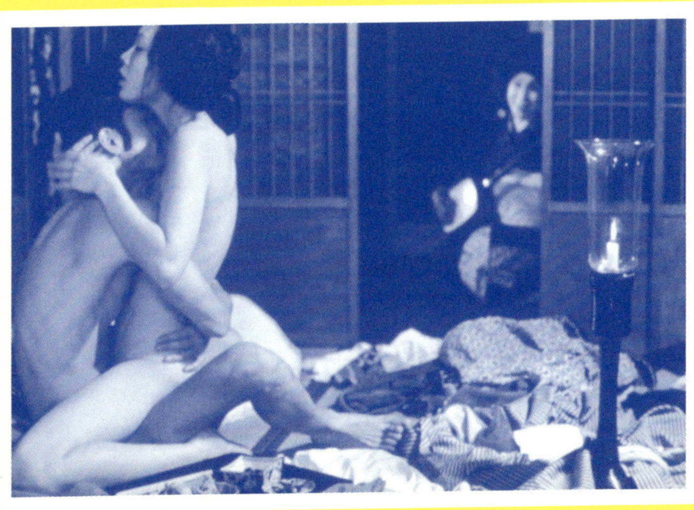

Nagisa Oshima, *In the Realm of the Senses*, 1976
Image courtesy of Janus Films

Freed to Love

from the more poetic title supplied by the movie's French producers.)

In the *Realm of the Senses* is almost exclusively concerned with unsimulated lovemaking between *Roman Porno* (romance pornography) actress Eiko Matsuda and Tatsuya Fuji, an established "straight" actor (if not as well-known as Marlon Brando). "It was unreasonable from the beginning to ask that the flow of acting be interrupted for sexual intercourse," Oshima wrote in the film's published script, suggesting that sex and rationality are by nature antithetical.

In the Realm of the Senses is a fundamentally avant-garde film. In its way, Oshima's paean to love is a successor to Carolee Schneemann's *Fuses* and Andy Warhol's still-proscribed *Blue Movie* (aka *Fuck*, 1969). That *In the Realm of the Senses* applies the structural repetition of Michael Snow's monumental *La Région Centrale* (1971) to some two hours of hardcore porn courts another sort of disorientation. (The titles of Snow's and Oshima's films are interchangeable.)

Certainly, Oshima was confident of his movie's world-historical significance. Citing his "unreasonable" demands placed on his cast, he observed that the fact that on-screen sexual intercourse performed by a famous actor with a normal family must be considered not only significant in the history of film, but also as the beginning of a new chapter in the annals of the history of sexual love in Japan or perhaps the world—because the taboos surrounding sexual intercourse that derive from the sacralization of monogamy system were thereby broken. The actress is not mentioned. One cannot help but note the apparent incongruity of a male director positing a movie climaxing with castration as the fulfillment of the sexual revolution. But, of course, unlike the lovemaking, the severing of star's member was not "real"—*In the Realm of the Senses* is a movie after all.

Hoberman

1.

Or to document. "Film directors want to shoot the dying," Nagisa Oshima wrote in the published screenplay for *In the Realm of the Senses*. "And they also want to shoot men and women (or men and men, women and women, or people and animals) having sexual intercourse."

2.

Underground satirist Robert Downey Sr. did as well, albeit to more comic effect, with his *No More Excuses*, a 1968 feature that cobbled together earlier and unfinished films, including outré footage from his commissioned softcore sex opus *The Sweet Smell of Sex* (naked fatties dry-humping to the theme from *A Man and a Woman*, a woman in bed with a chimpanzee), and, most interestingly, outtakes from a TV documentary on the then-new phenomenon of singles bars.

3.

The fourth-highest grossing movie of 1970, *B&C&T&A* won an Oscar for its screenplay (the National Society of Film Critics agreed). The two squares, Gould and Cannon, were both nominated for supporting roles and, as the movie's funnier and more sympathetic characters, were launched into stardom. In a way, they were more representative.

4.

The homosexual's "perverse condition" is disclosed in an hour-long series of tableaux, unified by voiceover narration and occasional dubbed dialogue. Images of self-absorption and sexual alienation are the essence of Praunheim's critique: homosexuals "compensate for their guilt feelings with an overdose of bourgeois virtues." They "live in a dream world of glossy magazines and Hollywood movies." They have made a cult of youth and physical appearances. Their "lifelong disappointment in love has made many of them cold and inhuman, so that the partner is only seen as a sex object."

5.

Still, it is not nearly as funny as Jim McBride's 1974 *Hot Times*, an almost Kucharesque piece of parody porn that, among other things, travesties the high school world of Archie comics while flipping the skin-flick scenario so that the movie is presented as a drama of teenage male sexual frustration.

Eric Schaefer

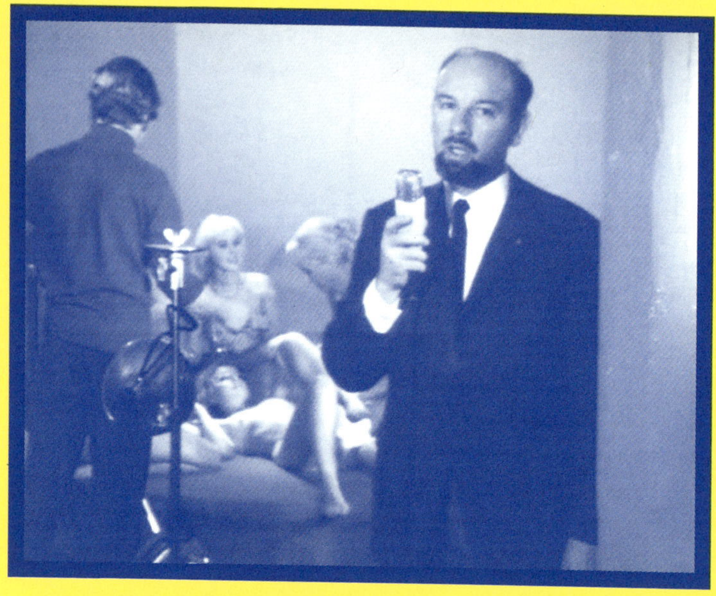

John Lamb, *Sexual Freedom in Denmark*, 1970

Freedom to Watch: Making the World Safe for Hardcore through Documentary

Future film historians will probably view with amusement the porno-docs, a pseudo genre of filmmaking that had its brief heyday in 1970. Industrious skin flickmakers and pornographers working from day to day in a constantly changing legal maze of U.S. Supreme Court decisions and local ordinances ingeniously wrapped their wares in a pseudo-journalistic "educational" format which the filmmaker-lawyers dictated to give hardcore material the legal elements of social redemption.[1]

If film historians have not found the porno-docs, such as *Red, White and Blue* written about in the 1971 review quoted above, that amusing, they do recognize them as important. The era of the strictly illegal stag film—seen only in clandestine venues such as fraternal lodges and brothels—had ended around 1969 as hardcore loops began to be shown in small storefront theaters, but it was not until *Deep Throat* created a cultural sensation in 1972 that the period of "porno chic" began. From 1969 to 1972 the documentary form helped make hardcore "safe" for those who made or watched pornography.

Education had been a key component of "adults-only" exploitation films since their emergence as theatrical fare in the late 1910s. The racy subjects and imagery that attended exploitation's topics (sex hygiene, prostitution, drugs, nudism) were justified through an educational imperative, often in the form of the "square-up," a moralistic title crawl that explained the necessity of exposing a social ill in all its lurid glory in order to combat it. Movies such as *Reefer Madness* (1936), *The Wages of Sin* (1938), and *She Shoulda Said 'No!'* (1948) relied on the square-up to foreground their pedagogic elements and insulate them from censorship and charges that they were merely trying to rake in a fast buck.[2]

Freedom to Watch

As nudie-cuties came to dominate the adults-only film in the
1960s, the educational trope diminished.

Changing attitudes about sex and the rise of sex education in schools precipitated the decline in the pedagogic
posture of exploitation films. Supreme Court rulings also
played a role. The court's Roth v. United States (1957) decision held that only obscenity was unprotected by the First
Amendment and that to be considered obscene "the average
person, applying contemporary community standards" had
to find that "the dominant theme of the material, taken as a
whole, appeals to prurient interest."[3] Writing in the Jacobellis
v. Ohio decision (1964), Justice William Brennan elaborated,
"material that deals with sex in a manner that advocates ideas,
or that has literary or scientific or artistic value or any other
form of social importance, may not be held obscene and
denied constitutional protection." These decisions pushed
producers of sexploitation films into more daring territory as
movies fused nudity with sexual situations in imports like
I, A Woman (1965), homegrown productions by well-known
directors like Russ Meyer, and assembly-line potboilers such
as *Brigitta* (1968). Eventually 16mm "simulation" films
included all of the movements of sexual intercourse, but body
positions or strategically placed bed sheets kept them from
straying into hardcore.[4]

The blue documentaries made between 1969 and 1972
were a significant bridge between softcore and hardcore
filmmaking, falling into several major categories. The first
were the marriage manual films, often called white-coaters
because they featured a physician figure serving as narrator and
on-screen docent. These films, such as *Man and Wife* (1969)
and *Kama Sutra '71* (1970), included information about
sexuality with performers demonstrating different techniques
and positions. The second type of film was the sociological
documentary that addressed changes in sex and society, such

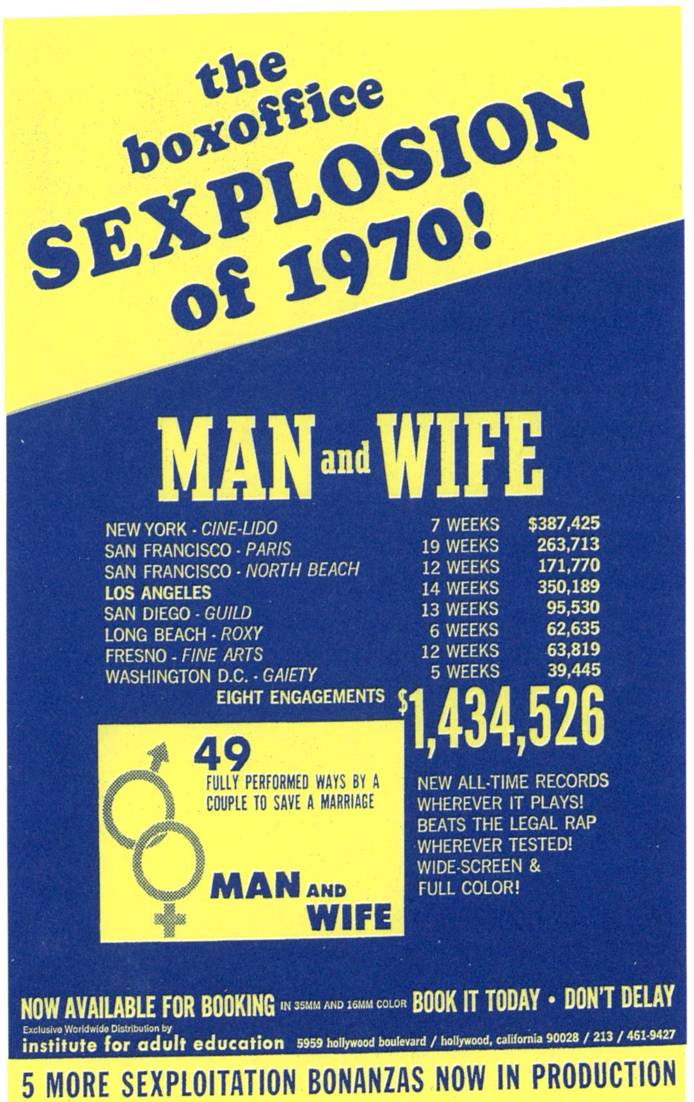

Poster for *Man and Wife*, 1969

Freedom to Watch

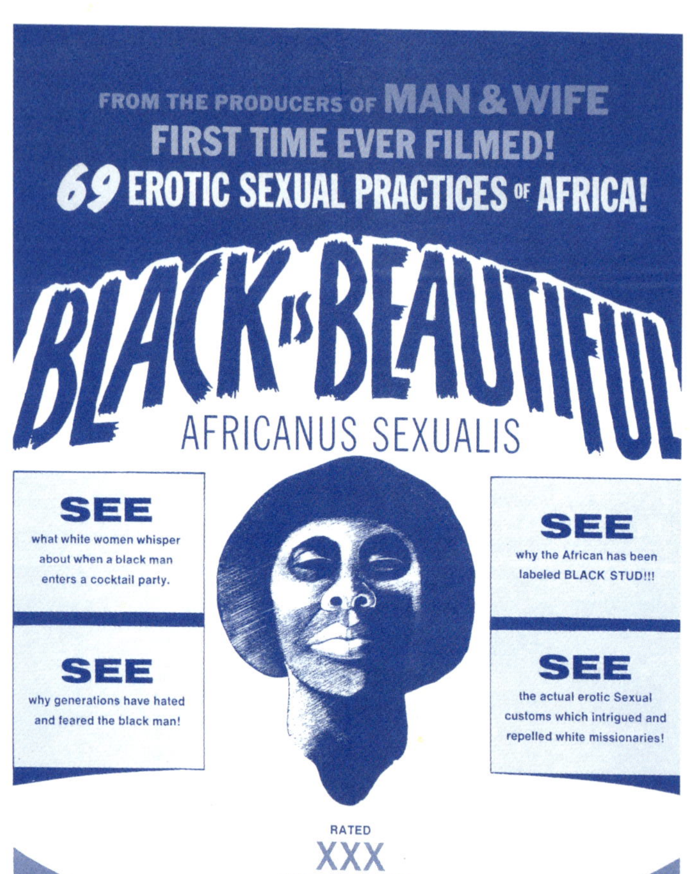

Poster for *Africanus Sexualis* (aka *Black is Beautiful*), 1970

as *American Sexual Revolution* and *Pornography Prostitution USA* (both 1971). The last category was the historical film, such as the unambiguously titled *History of the Blue Movie* (1970) and *Erotography* (1971), a survey of erotica through the ages. Some, such as *Sexual Freedom in Denmark* (1970), combined categories.[5]

The gambit of employing documentary tactics was not lost on critics. David Denby opined in the *Atlantic Monthly* in 1970, "The stately and portentous documentary form may be ideally suited to anxious pornographers; 'redeeming social commentary' is built into the structure, no matter what the subject."[6] He cited Alex de Renzy's *Pornography in Denmark* (1970) as "tricked out with all the documentary apparatus—quotes from experts, man-in-the-street interviews"—but labeled it "disingenuous and trashy" and concluded, "it should get by in court." While *Pornography in Denmark's* motives might have been questioned, other critics recognized that it delivered the goods. A review in *Boxoffice* pronounced that it "removed any restrictions regarding what sexual activity may be shown on screen."[7] Hardcore imagery required a justification, and the documentary form provided it by advocating ideas and making claims to scientific or social importance.

The porn documentary bandwagon was crowded as individuals jostled for a spot onboard. They included dirty book publisher Marvin Miller, who teamed with director Matt Cimber's New World Studios to distribute films through the high-minded-sounding Institute for Adult Education.[8] In quick succession they cranked out three white-coaters: *Man and Wife* (1969), *He and She* (1970), and *Africanus Sexualis* (aka *Black Is Beautiful*, 1970). For the release of *The Sensually Liberated Female* in 1971, the Institute wrote to film bookers—evidently with no irony—"one of the most knowledgeable and expensive agencies researched this film in order to reach the maximum penetration in your local market."[9]

Freedom to Watch

John Lamb, who produced the first nudist feature with both full-frontal male and female nudity, *The Raw Ones* (1965), headed to Europe to make *Sexual Freedom in Denmark* (1970), followed by *Sexual Freedom Now!* (1971). Sexploitation stalwart David F. Friedman produced *Red, White and Blue* (1971), an exegesis on the Commission on Obscenity and Pornography. De Renzy, a San Francisco hardcore pioneer, made three widely released documentaries in 1970 alone: *Pornography in Denmark: A New Approach* (aka *Censorship in Denmark*), *A History of the Blue Movie*, and *Sexual Encounter Group*. And before he made the groundbreaking *Deep Throat* in 1972, Gerard Damiano directed porn documentaries, including *The Marriage Manual* and *Changes* (both 1970) and *Sex USA* (1971). The years 1970 and 1971 alone saw the release of at least three dozen blue documentaries.

Then there were the Kronhausens. Next to Masters and Johnson, Phyllis and Eberhard Kronhausen were the most famous couple in the field of sexuality in the 1960s.[10] If Masters and Johnson provided the stern face of hard sexual science in their lab coats, the Kronhausens were the warm and fuzzy sweater-clad spokespersons for humanistic sexology. For a time the Kronhausens were everywhere. They co-wrote books including *Pornography and the Law* (1959), *Sex Histories of American College Men* (1960), and *The Sexually Responsive Woman* (1964), as well as volumes on erotic fantasies, performers, bookplates, and art. Drawing from their own collection, the self-described "erotologists" organized the first public exhibition of erotic art in Sweden in 1968 and later opened The International Museum of Erotic Art in San Francisco.[11] They made experimental films, documentaries, and a pornographic feature; contributed articles to magazines; and palled around with celebrities such as Erica Jong, author of the sexy bestseller *Fear of Flying* (1973); photographer Diane Arbus; and actress Shirley MacLaine.[12]

Schaefer

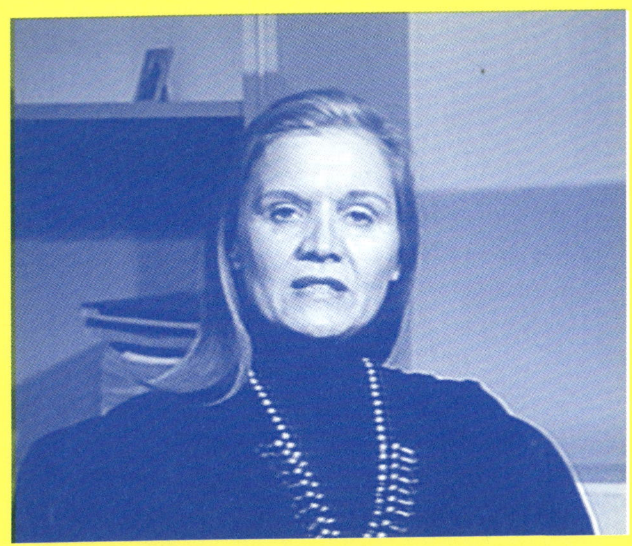

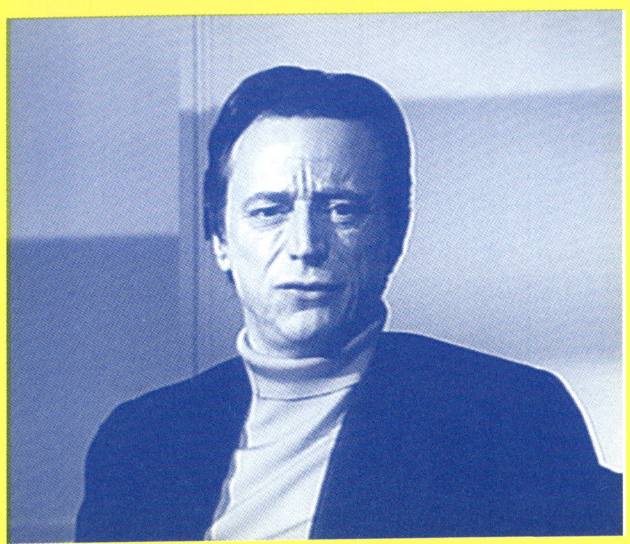

Phyllis & Eberhard Kronhausen

Freedom to Watch

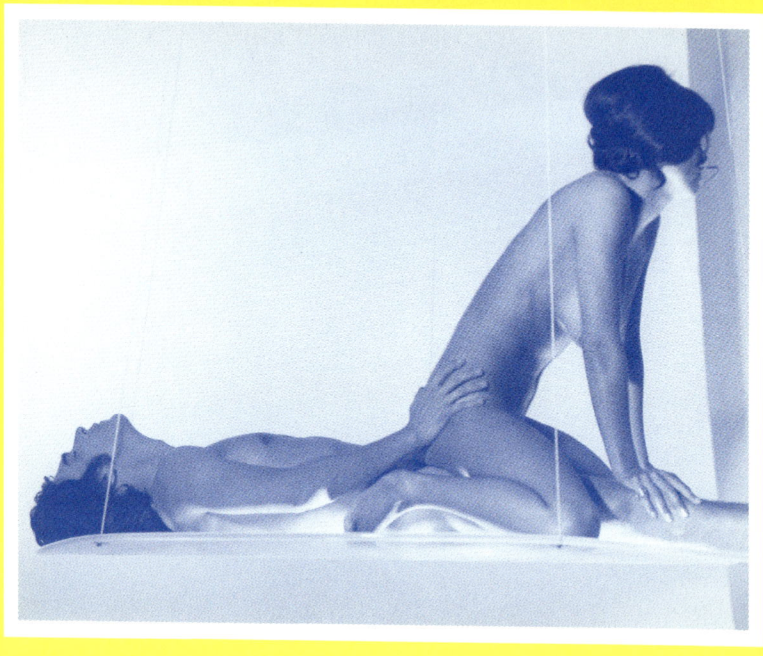

Eric Jeffrey Haims, *101 Acts of Love*, 1970

By all rights, their documentary *Freedom to Love* (1969) should have been a hit.

The Kronhausens situated their own celebrity at the center of *Freedom to Love*, serving as an echo chamber as they agreed with each other about censorship and sex laws. (Eberhard: "The question, really, is whether we should have any sex laws at all?" Phyllis: "I don't see why we should have very many of them."[13]) They served as on-screen interlocutors for *Playboy* publisher Hugh Hefner, feminist artist Betty Dodson, critic Kenneth Tynan, and the chief of the British Board of Film Censors, John Trevelyan. Scenes from the plays *The Beard* (1965) and *Geese* (1969) were presented, and the film dramatized incidents involving a young man who discovers his lover is underage, two adolescent girls who spy on a pair of lesbians and then conduct their own sexual experiments, and a climactic group sex party.

Ultimately *Freedom to Love* was done in by several factors. While *Variety* found it to be a "sincere" document, it noted the movie's lack of technical polish and the "self-consciously casual conversation between the therapists."[14] Beyond this, its broad-brush approach—hopscotching between the United States, Great Britain, and European countries, and flipping between interviews and reenactments—made it disjointed. Its American distributor, Grove Press Films, had already expended a huge amount of capital defending *I Am Curious (Yellow)* (1967) in the courts, so promotional efforts were fairly minimal. Finally, *Freedom to Love* trailed *Pornography in Denmark*, *Sexual Freedom in Denmark*, and a number of white-coaters into theaters, making it rather passé by the time it opened.

Even if *Freedom to Love* failed to hit it big, the combined educational and prurient appeal of other porn docs proved to be a winning formula. *Man and Wife* grossed over $1.4 million from only eight engagements in spring of 1970.

Freedom to Watch

Sexual Freedom in Denmark grossed $1.9 million in 1970, which *Variety* noted "accounted for better than one-half of 1% of the entire US market" for the year.[15] It also put the film ahead of *Chisum* with John Wayne and the Clint Eastwood war film *Kelly's Heroes*, among other mainstream offerings. Runs of weeks—sometimes months—were frequent, and the documentaries had the capacity to break out of the grindhouse ghetto to play in legitimate showcase theaters around the country.

Despite their educational bona fides, the blue docs were not without controversy. A New York criminal court declared *Pornography in Denmark* obscene and it was pulled from the 55th Street Playhouse—only to be replaced by *Man and Wife*.[16] *A History of the Blue Movie*, *The Postgraduate*, and *Sexual Freedom in Denmark* were also busted in New York City, while the Maryland state censors attempted to bar *Black is Beautiful* and *Freedom to Love*.[17] Meanwhile, *Man and Wife* was prosecuted in Miami, St. Louis, and Columbus, Ohio, among other cities. US Customs held up *The Language of Love* (1969), an early Swedish entry in the field. The ensuing court proceedings lasted for nearly two years, and by the time it was finally released in 1971, the porn-doc craze was fizzling. This was in no small measure due to the increasingly wide release of quality narrative hardcore features such as *Mona: The Virgin Nymph* (1970), *Adultery for Fun and Profit* (1971), and *School Girl* (1971).

The porn docs suffered many problems: low budgets, poor direction, boring stretches, an affectation of importance. They were also saddled with the shortcomings of conventional documentaries. They relied on experts of various stripes and grounded their discourse in authority when the sexual liberation movement had an anti-authoritarian impulse. Their use of on- or off-screen narrators made them seem pedantic

Schaefer

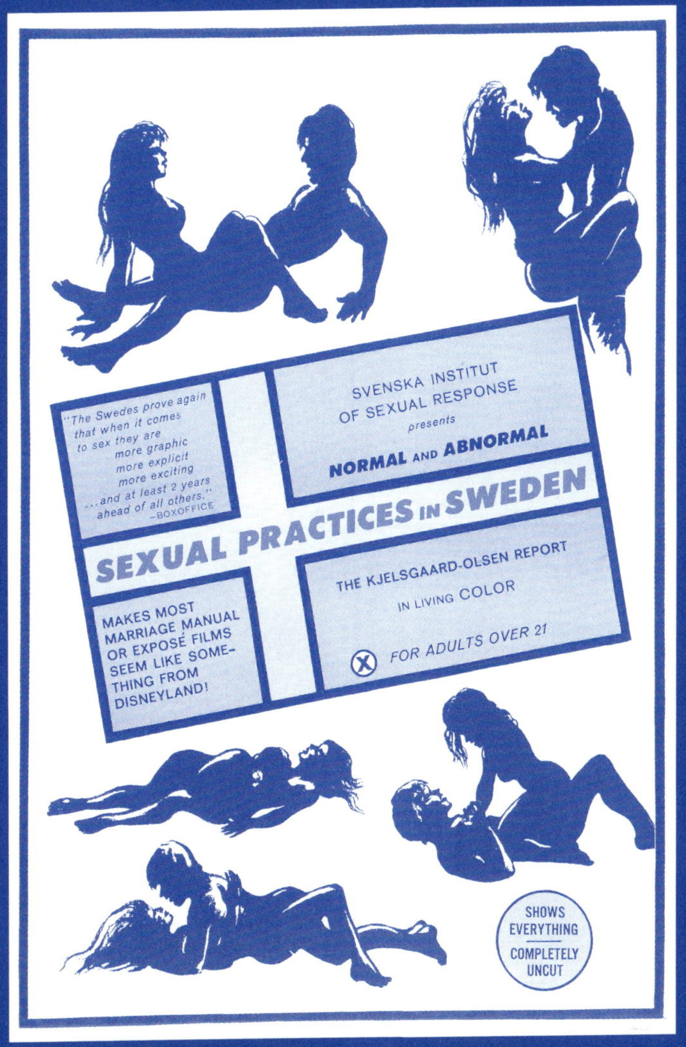

Poster for *Sexual Practices in Sweden*, 1970

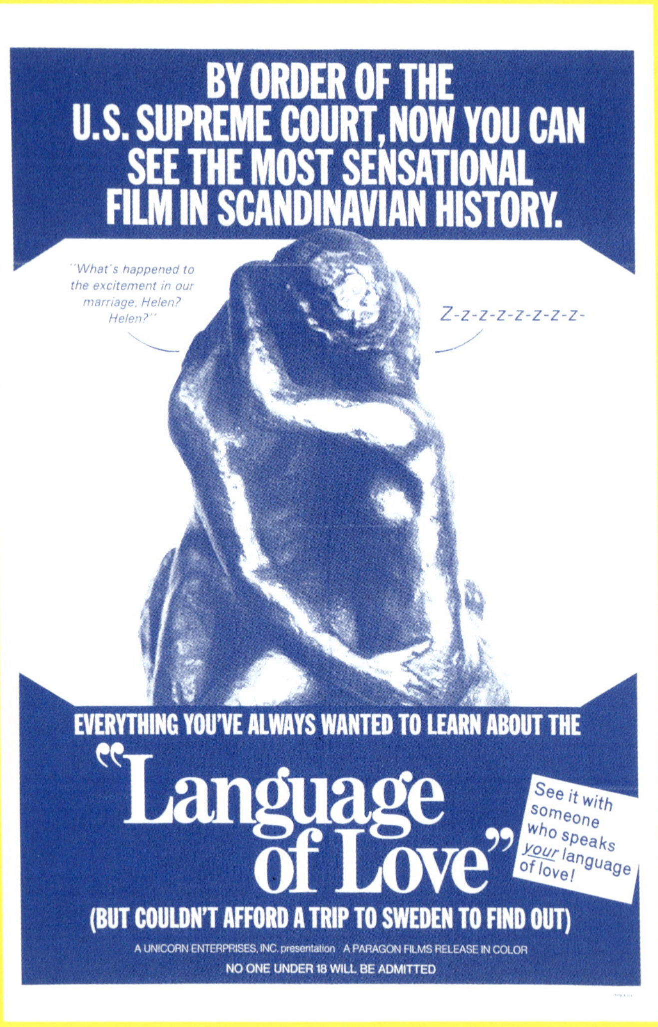

Poster for *Langauge of Love*, 1969

and stuffy. Traditional documentary techniques that marked them as "educational," allowing them to claim "social relevance," also served to drain the blood and cool the heat of the blue docs. And if the documentary form was, to a large extent, concerned with reality and rectitude, that put it in direct conflict with pornography's goals: to create fantasy and frisson. No matter that bodies were engaging in hardcore sexual action on screen, having someone intone, "The prerequisite of physical arousal including erection and lubrication of the male and female genital organs is seen to be of utmost importance," blunted any erotic effect.[18] The impulse to make hardcore action respectable via the documentary form also made it profoundly un-erotic. And this was precisely what the sexual liberation movement, which porn allegedly exemplified, was not supposed to be.

Had the makers of porn docs adopted the fly-on-the-wall, observational style of Direct Cinema emerging in the 1960s, the porn doc might have had more long-term viability. Although narrative came to dominate in the "golden age" of hardcore in the 1970s and into the 1980s, today much internet porn (including the "casting," "P.O.V." and "homemade" subgenres) hews to a documentary or "reality" structure, even if it has little relationship with the early blue docs. And yet it was those early, often dry and pedantic porn documentaries that forged the path for the adult entertainment we take for granted today.

Freedom to Watch

1.
Rick, Review of *Red, White and Blue*, *Variety*, 3 March 1971, 22.

2.
For a full history of early exploitation, see Eric Schaefer, *"Bold! Daring! Shocking! True!": A History of Exploitation Films, 1919–1959* (Durham, NC: Duke University Press, 1999). A more concise discussion of the education/exploitation nexus can be found in Schaefer, "Exploitation as Education," in *Learning with the Lights Off: Educational Film in the United States*, ed. Devin Orgeron, Marsha Orgeron, and Dan Streible (New York: Oxford University Press, 2012), 316–37.

3.
For the text of Roth, see http://www.law.cornell.edu/supct/html/historics/USSC_CR_0354_0476_ZS.html (accessed 12 August 2013). For the text of Jacobellis, see http://www.law.cornell.edu/supremecourt/text/378/184 (accessed 12 August 2013).

4.
See Eric Schaefer, "Gauging a Revolution: 16mm Film and the Rise of the Pornographic Feature," *Cinema Journal* 41, no. 3 (Spring 2002), 3–26.

5.
The first half of *Sexual Freedom in Denmark* dealt with changes in pornography laws in Denmark in 1968 and 1969. The second half included sequences on anatomy, the mechanics of coitus, venereal disease, and childbirth. John Lamb's distribution company, Art Films International, received numerous requests from medical schools, colleges, and religious groups requesting the "clinical" portion of the film for use in training, and the company provided access to 16mm prints to such institutions for several years. John Lamb Papers, collection of the author.

6.
David Denby, "Dirty Movies—Hard and Soft," *Atlantic Monthly*, August 1970, 101.

7.
"A New Approach to Censorship in Denmark" [review of *Pornography in Denmark*], *Boxoffice*, 29 June 1970, n.p.

8.
This company is not to be confused with Roger Corman's New World Pictures, founded in 1971.

9.

Richard Frank, "To Our Valued Customer," undated promotional letter, collection of the author.

10.

Although variously referred to as "psychologists" and "psycho-therapists," the good doctors held Ed.D.s from the Teachers College at Columbia University.

11.

"Eros Explored," *New York Times*, 4 August 1968. The museum closed two years later due to a lack of funds.

12.

The Kronhausens eventually put aside their credentials as warriors in the sexual revolution to write a book about antioxidants and diet, and later ran a bed and breakfast in Costa Rica. They returned to New York, where Eberhard died in 2009 at the age of 94. Phyllis died at 83 in 2012. Despite their renown in the 1960s and '70s, they failed to warrant obituaries in the *New York Times* or other national publications.

13.

Dialogue from *Freedom to Love*.

14.

Verr, Review of *Freedom to Love*, *Variety*, 17 June 1970, 16.

15.

"U.S. Films' Share-Of-Market Profile," *Variety*, 12 May 1971, 36.

16.

"Adversary Hearing; Sherpix to Trial; Three House Managers Menaced," *Variety*, 7 October 1970, 4.

17.

"Sherpix Key Case Now Set for Jan. 11," *Variety*, 16 December 1970, 5; "Maryland Censors Lose on Pair," *Variety*, 2 June 1971, 23.

18.

Narration from *Sexual Freedom in Denmark*.

Elena Gorfinkel

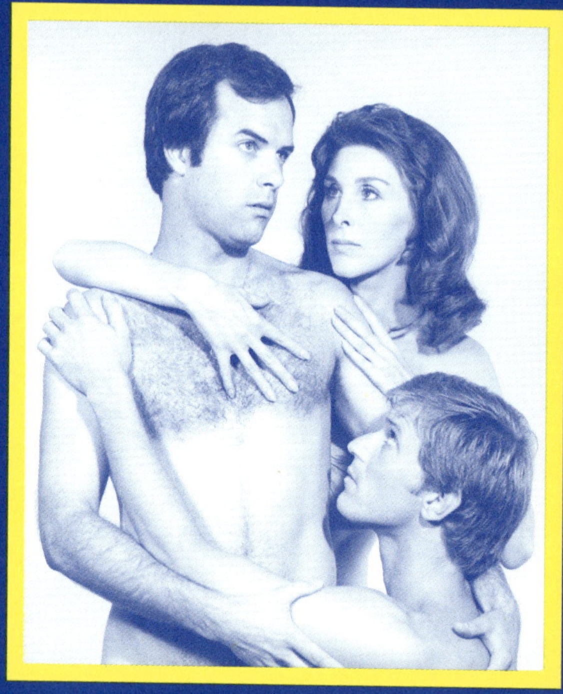

Radley Metzger, *Score*, 1972
Images courtesy Audubon Films

Seduction Time: Radley Metzgers' "Score" and the Utopian Gesture

Radley Metzger's *Score* (1972) is perhaps one of the most utopian sex films of its era, a self-professed adult fairytale that occurs "once upon a future time." The film presents the story of two married couples—libertine swingers Elvira and Jack and young innocents Betsy and Eddie—who embark on an evening of same-sex seduction. Taking place over the course of a single day, charmingly buoyant in its dialogue, and scored to the refrain of an infectious unknown rock song, "Where is the Girl," Metzger based the film on the off-Broadway play of the same name by Jerry Douglas. The free-loving Elvira (Claire Wilbur) makes a wager with her husband Jack (Gerald Grant) that she can seduce the naive Betsy (Lynn Lowry). The bet is part of an ongoing, playful agon between the couple, measured by their successful seductions and sexual conquests over the last six months. Thus the titular keeping of a score, and the "score" itself, is timed to a deadline, an inbuilt apparatus of suspense: the virtuous Betsy must be "achieved" by the stroke of midnight. Timing is everything in this compressed romp, particularly in the anticipation of the pleasure yet to come. Innuendo, double entendre, barely veiled implications, seemingly innocent suggestions, all point to the slowly developing telos of erotic release and the grander design of Elvira and Jack's game, one that is as contingent on the frisson of limitation and restriction, on the challenge of the chase, as it is on an idea of untrammeled freedom. By the end of the evening, a night replete with the playtime of dressing-up in costumes (sailor, cowboy, harlot, nun), dancing, smoking pot, and sniffing poppers, Betsy has succumbed to the ministrations of Elvira, while the closeted Eddie (Cal Culver) has fallen into the firm embrace of the bemused Jack.

Score's timing and timeliness is as much formal as it is historical. It occupies a unique place in the history of adult cinema and sexual representation of the late 1960s and early 1970s. It is a distillation of the complex transformations of the sexual revolution and a fundamentally queer text that imbibes, with breezy finesse, the idealist spirit of the era's aspirations to sexual egalitarianism. The film is at once a sexploitation film made on the cusp of the arrival of hardcore feature-length pornography and an art film that presents an intensely modulated sexual parlor game. *Score* thus embodies the hybridity of its director's oeuvre, his location between art house, sexploitation, and pornographic filmmaking modes.

Metzger's status in the emerging adult cinema of the 1960s as the most prominent maker and distributor of erotic films in this period is well documented but often under examined in film histories of the industry and screen sex. A lifelong cinephile, Metzger began his film career in the 1950s as a freelance editor, notably editing the late neorealist film *Bitter Rice* (1949, Giuseppe DiSantis) for its US release at RKO, and later cutting trailers for Bergman, Antonioni, and Truffaut films in the late 1950s and early 1960s at Janus Films.[1] Metzger left Janus to start the production and distribution house Audubon Films with his business partner, Ava Leighton, as they bought and distributed many racy imports (sometimes with inserted, newly shot footage) for the burgeoning US art-house market—films such as *Mademoiselle Striptease* (1959/63), *Sweet Ecstasy*, with Elke Sommer (1962), *Sexus* (1965), and *The Libertine* (1969).

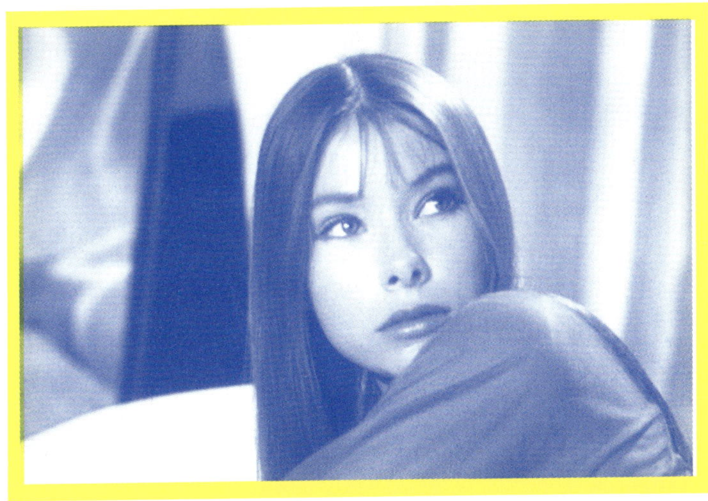

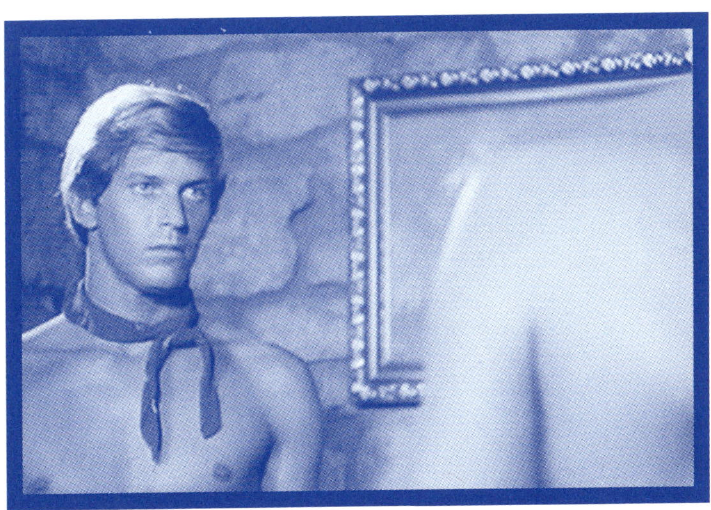

Seduction Time

Their distribution of the Swedish import *I, A Woman* (US 1966, Mac Ahlberg), starring the fulsome Essy Persson, was an erotic film landmark which made over $3 million in its US release; it did a considerable amount to expand the sex film market toward more "upscale" venues beyond those of the grindhouse.[2] Audubon widened sexploitation's predominantly male audience base to include women, couples, and hipper, younger audiences, elevating the status of and imparting a certain seriousness to the lowly category of the sex film.

Dubbed an "aristocrat of the erotic" by critics and industry observers in the 1960s, Metzger made contributions to American film culture with his hybridization of two distinct modes of production: the imported art film with its complex, ambivalent characters and frank, adult themes, and the sexploitation film, produced by a proliferating cottage industry in the US that parlayed low-budget erotic potboilers leavened with female nudity and a leering, illicit address towards sexual subjects. In his own films, Metzger's aesthetic approach and moral stance on sexuality remained decidedly permissive and Continental. By the late 1960s, his film budgets also far exceeded the $20–40,000 per-picture average of sexploitation films, and his European locations, international name actors, and modern set design and extravagant costumes attested to an industry practice that was clearly aligned with the pedigree of the art cinema. One can readily see the affinity of Metzger's films to the contemplative, conceptual tone of Alain Resnais mixed with the pop lustiness of Roger Vadim—far more than a resemblance to his bawdy, brash sexploitation contemporaries Russ Meyer or David Friedman. Metzger's comparably opulent films, in their attention to the travails and subjectivities of the upper classes, often deployed the adaptation and erotic modernization of literary sources—Prosper Merimee's *Carmen von Carmen, Baby* (1967), Alexandre Dumas II's *The Lady of the Camellias* in *Camille 2000* (1969) and Violette Leduc's novel of the same name in *Therese and Isabelle* (1969). These films honed their focus on the erotics of the existential over the economic, and prioritized the charmingly disaffected rather than the sensational desperation of the down-and-out. The tropes of female desire, subjectivity, and longing, as well as the drama of non-normative object choices, particularly lesbianism, were a central component of Metzger's oeuvre, presaging his foray into bisexuality and same-sex experimentation in *Score*.

Shot in 1972 in Yugoslavia, and released in late 1973, *Score* had to find its niche in the trailing wake of "porno chic," heralded most notoriously with the widespread exhibition of Gerard Damiano's *Deep Throat* (1972). Despite legal rulings and public consternation, the hardcore feature was becoming a permanent fixture in the cultural landscape. This sea change in movies' sexual explicitness was altering conceptions of public and private spheres, proper and improper film tastes, permissible and impermissible desires. Located at this historical juncture between softcore and hardcore filmmaking, *Score* signals the end of an era for Metzger, as one of his last softcore films. He would subsequently transition into pseudonymous hardcore film production as Henry Paris, directing now-esteemed porn classics such as *The Private Afternoons of Pamela Mann* (1974), *The Opening of Misty Beethoven* (1976), and *Barbara Broadcast* (1977).

One of the first films to generously present bisexuality right at the cusp of the arrival of "bisexual chic," as announced by *Newsweek* in 1974, and in an era of gay liberation, *Score* was also perched between straight and gay adult cinemas. *Score* was released in softcore and hardcore versions, the latter geared to appeal to gay audiences and

YOU'VE BEEN READING ABOUT THE BI-SEXUAL CHIC PHENOMENON

"Metzger's major sex scenes, which describe the intitiation into bisexuaⁱⁱty of a naive young couple by an experienced older one, have a flow, and erotic rhythm and an intensity greater than most sex you see on film. The sex, instead of being presented as something remarkable in itself (which, in 1974, is hardly the case) has been given imaginative, compelling cinematic form. It makes voyeurism seem artistic."

Howard Kissel/*WOMEN'S WEAR DAILY*

"Radley Metzger has outdone himself with 'SCORE'. It has performers of chic and muscle, and a plot securely tied to the long suspense of seduction. Lest you think that all this has diluted the essential porn, be comforted. It's all there; male and female, female and female, male and male. The 'X' rating is richly deserved."

Archer Winsten/*N.Y. POST*

"It's titillating! You could go see 'Score' with a friend, have lots of laughs and draw some interesting conclusions."

Liz Smith/*COSMOPOLITAN*

" 'SCORE' gives you more!" Frances Taylor/*L.I. PRESS*

"Something for everybody." Arthur Knight/
PLAYGIRL MAGAZINE

"Swinging both ways is the new wrinkle explored by Metzger."
Bruce Williamson/*PLAYBOY*

"Will appeal to just about any sexual appetite." –*ADVOCATE*

"Metzger explores a world of textures, sounds and colors, each complimenting the other, all part of the visual, aural, sexual experience...leaves everyone sexually charged."
GALLERY MAGAZINE

"Radley Metzger has pulled a neat trick in making this well written, well photographed film a triple A — adult, amusing and artistic."
Norma Mclain Stoop/*AFTER DARK*

"Radley Metzger hilariously hits the bulls eye of Bi-sexual chic — a guaranteed turn on for any audience."
Robert Weiner/
*INTERVIEW/
ZOO WORLD*

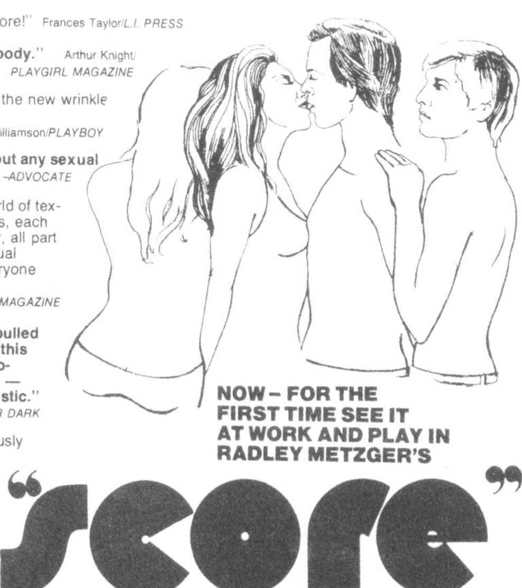

With Claire Wilbur/Calvin Culver/Lynn Lowry/Gerald Grant/Carl Parker
Screenplay by Jerry Douglas/Eastmancolor/Directed by Radley Metzger
an Audubon Films Release/In Color

included an extra seven minutes of male frontal nudity and explicit sex performed by the openly gay Grant and Culver. Culver had just appeared, as Casey Donovan, in Wakefield Poole's hallmark gay hardcore film *Boys in the Sand* (1971), and he would go on to star in Jerry Douglas' *The Back Row* (1973), among many others that decade. *Score* may have suffered at the box office due to its risky and progressive paralleling of male and female bisexuality; the predominantly straight male sexploitation public was a tough sell, whereas "women respond[ed] to that footage," as reported in an account of Audubon's different campaigns for the film.[3] Both swinging and bisexuality were certainly afoot in other mid-range films of the time: in Paul Mazursky's *Bob & Carol & Ted & Alice* (1969) and John Schlesinger's *Sunday Bloody Sunday* (1971), films undoubtedly more realist, equivocating, and far less explicitly sexual than *Score*.

What perhaps defines *Score* the most strongly is its quality of a cinephilic time capsule, a carefree confection of the fantasy of erotic transformation, particularly that experienced by Betsy and Eddie. The narrative of trans-formation is also central to a liberatory discourse of sexuality of the era. *Score*, in its optimism and lightness, establishes a particular tone unique for adult cinema of the time. On the one hand, its intellectual seriousness allies it with a libertine pedagogy à la Sade's *Philosophy of the Bedroom*, yet its humor and comic styling recall the innuendo and repartee of Hollywood screwball comedy and the bourgeois farce of Ernst Lubitsch. The intellectual stakes of Metzger's erotics are here most readily unveiled: he is fundamentally a fantasist, something also made eminently clear by one of his prior films, *The Lickerish Quartet* (1970), a treatise on projection, fantasy, and the mutability of cinematic experience, filtered through Pirandello and Pasolini's *Teorema* (1968). It is precisely in the sphere of fantasy—whose apogee

Seduction Time

one could claim is the cinema—that the utopian possibility of autonomous erotic expression can be achieved.

Consider the opening sexual triangulation that serves as the prelude to Betsy's later seduction. Elvira pretends the phone line is broken, and has Jack call the telephone company. The worried Betsy, who had been trying to call, comes over to chat with Elvira, inquiring about their taste for swinging. Jack and Elvira had put an ad in a paper and hooked up with a tourist couple the night before, and their house is still mussed with the traces of last night's sex party. The telephone man, Mike Nixon (the axiomatically masculine Carl Parker), arrives to fix the phone line, and Elvira mounts her offensive. While salaciously talking up the repairman, she trips Betsy as she passes him his coffee, and the unraveling begins. The repairman's soaked shirt comes off, cream must be procured to lubricate the burn on his chest, more clothes are removed as Elvira and Mike get horizontal on the shag rug, all while Betsy watches from the corner of the room, Jack's Polaroid camera in hand. We have thus moved with speed and ease, in Sadean fashion, from the explication to the demonstration of libertinage, all in the interest of staging a scene to pique Betsy–who had just an hour or two earlier been rebuffed by Eddie in their marital bed. Curious yet unschooled, not knowing how to look at what she sees, yet not wanting to look away, Betsy clicks the Polaroid and takes a picture just as Elvira and Mike vigorously roll on the shag rug and fuck, reaching orgasm. There is a sharp cut right at the moment of the click, to across town, as Jack's photo shoot (he is a professional photographer of "nudes") climaxes as his model high-dive splashes into the water. This architectonic yet incredibly buoyant series of actions provides a particular kind of delight—the pleasure taken in the rhythmic pacing of its design, a telos of erotic causality, as well as the ramification of the metatextual frame and of the "corrupted"

Gorfinkel

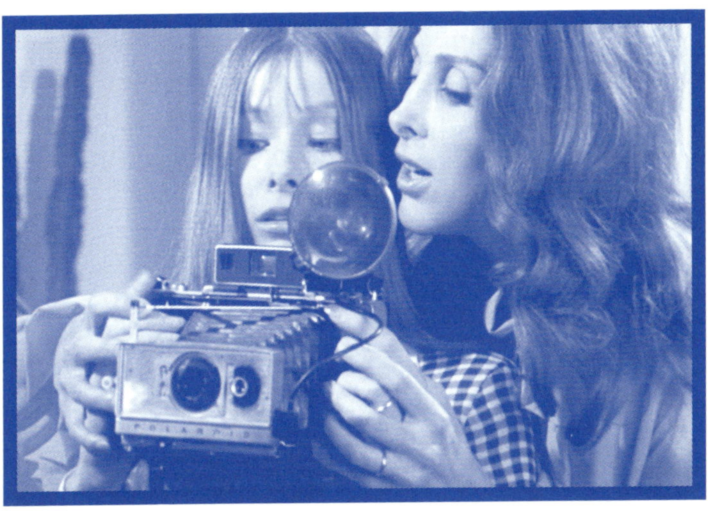

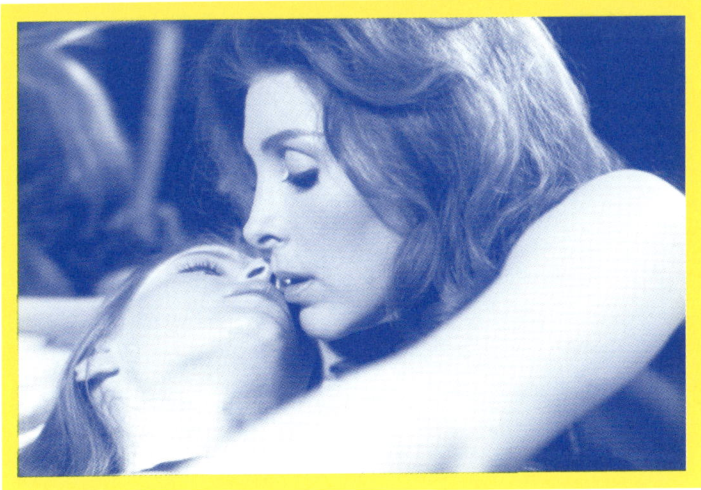

Seduction Time

spectator, Betsy, who, by looking, "frames" the action. One sexual action sets off another and then another, until the momentum cannot be arrested or stalled, and Betsy, the erotic initiate of *Score*, must enter the sexual scene, the frame of the fantasy itself. *Score* thus enacts the timing— the suspense, the anticipation—of seduction, as well as its intimacy, fragility, and psychological and corporeal intensity. The will to seduce is also coextensive with a willingness to be seduced, and *Score* shrewdly recognizes this irony. The film's essential modernity aligns with its fablelike and fabulated premise, creating out of erotic aspiration something unequivocally more abstract.

Metzger's late-1960s films elaborated an aesthetic indebted to the hallowed mise-en-scene tradition of Max Ophuls and Josef von Sternberg; Richard Corliss vividly remarked that "Metzger's intentions to become the Ophuls of orgasm, the concupiscent Cukor, are the most appealing aspects of the man and his gaudily proficient films."[4] The extravagances of a lush mise-en-scene, ornate set design, and striking compositions pulse throughout Metzger's cinema, and he once noted that it was Jean Renoir who impressed upon him that "there's just one moment that people remember in a film and that's enough."[5] This credo becomes a hyperbolic axiom, as *Therese*, *Camille*, and *Carmen* are full of arresting shots, refracting images, and vibratory fragments, overflowing with the decorative surplus that incited disdain as well as admiration from his critics. For example, we can recall the way in which Metzger films bodies through glass bottles in *Carmen*, and, in *Camille 2000*, how he employs a minimalist, pneumatic, white mod set with clear plastic bed and refracting mirrors and dramatizes Camille's orgasm through a rack focus between a close-up of Danielle Gaubert's face and a vase of camellias.

Gorfinkel

In *Score*, this precedent of sumptuous production design is considerably scaled back, yet an aesthetic decadence is still at work. Shot on the Dalmatian coast of Yugoslavia to resemble a luxurious Riviera-ish resort town, the film's modest budget and less lavish settings facilitated a closer focus on the actor's performing bodies and a tighter shooting style and framing than the long shots prevalent in Metzger's prior films. Metzger made liberal use of selective focus, using a shallow depth of field and alternating between characters in medium close-up as a means of accentuating the febrile nature of an as-yet-unconsummated sexual encounter. Faces and crotches, upper and lower extremities are often placed together in a post-*Graduate* framing mélange which manipulates the depth and spatial relations of an image. Metzger also served as the principal camera operator on this film, one of the only instances that he would take on the directing and cinematography, which yields a particular quality of intimacy between camera and subjects—particularly in the scenes between Culver and Grant, at one point in which the camera appears attached to Grant's posterior in the softcore version of the film, both showing yet still withholding the spectacle of fellatio.

The sprightly and clever editorial organization develops a quickening pace as the film develops, and it never lets an image lag or expire. Metzger's style shows itself most radically through its use of two staples of cinematic continuity, shot-reverse shot and cross-cutting, the latter in patterns that connect the sexual action happening upstairs and downstairs, as Elvira's "Operation Musicbox" accelerates. Building an intensifying domino game out of finely wrought close-ups, which suggest the intoxicating flirtation of a boozy encounter in which bodies are rendered in their encroaching closeness to each other, the editing highlights Metzger's capacity to carve cinematic space out of flesh, among other

Seduction Time

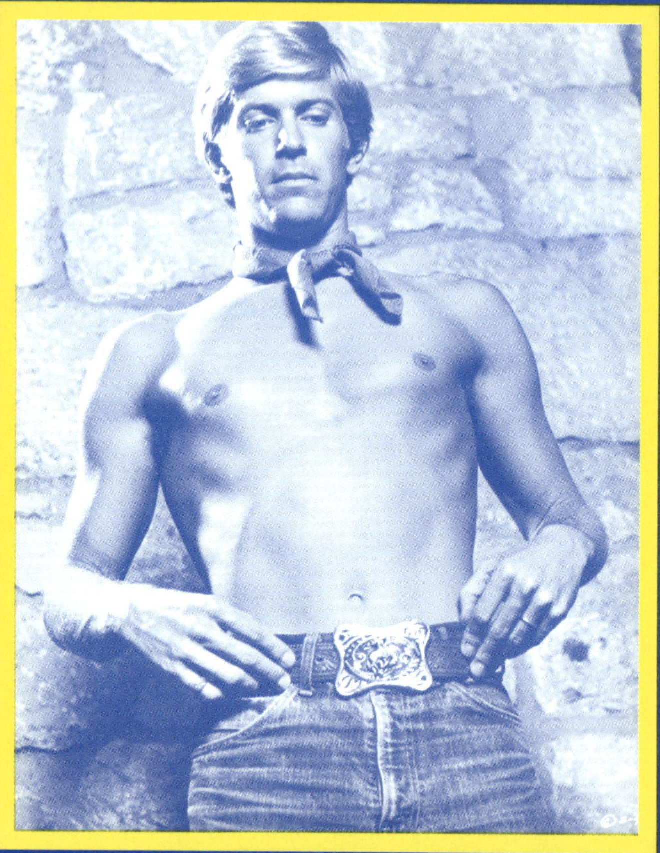

material, profilmic elements. The archly regal Wilbur, the tanned and stolid Grant, the childishly petulant Lowry, and the homespun, all-American Culver offer up their features, their poised, expectant faces, and the agile extremities of their bodies, in concert with the plentiful decorative things, those cinematic objects and props which so often take a great part in the erotic congress mobilizing Metzger's filmic compositions. Numerous images resonate with an eroticization of that which exists just out of frame. The handover of the jeans for Eddie's cowboy costume, for example, rests on a visual pun in which the V shape of the denim's legs, held upside down by Jack, becomes a come-on gesture, signaling Jack's desire and Eddie's nakedness. The consummating sex scene between the two men contains a striking shot in which the empty frame is penetrated by a pointy red object, slow moving into the center of the image. We realize that it is the red bandana that has been tied by Jack around Eddie's neck, a sartorial appendage reflecting Eddie's desired self—the cowboy, his masculine ego ideal—and an erect signifier that precedes an oncoming open-mouthed kiss between the two as their faces slowly inhabit and take over the composition.

In these myriad instants, *Score* constructs the visual pleasure of erotic synchronicity via a deftly manipulated mise-en-scene and the precision of montage. As with Metzger's earlier films, mirrors, plants, glass objects, sculptures, rugs, and other textural elements brush up against or partly obscure the bodies maneuvering around each other in the shot. Producing a thicket of textures within the frame itself, an unstripped image layered with seductive scrims, screens, reflections, and chromatic filters, *Score* pulsates with the vibrant density of an extended aesthetic of forepleasure. Early in the film, a closeup shot of coffee cups being stirred at contrasting speeds, by Elvira and Betsy, acts as a prelude to other forms of possible sexual synchronicity. After their

Seduction Time

dinner, the pulsing lights of a disco ball and spectrum light chromatically diffuse the two couples' faces in tints of red, blue, and green. A tent-shaped mirror over Elvira's bed creates a space of enclosure, mirroring Betsy's beseeching face, upending and refracting her plaintive curiosity and self-questioning. And one of the most visually emblematic scenes of *Score* features a wave machine that cuts across the frame and blocks off Elvira and Betsy's faces as they talk on either side of the sculptural object in shot-reverse shot. The distorted transparency between Elvira's and Betsy's faces, the rocking to and fro of the blue viscous fluid, becomes an allegory for the swaying play, the opacity of desire, the narrowing gulf of what is as yet unspoken between them. This fusion of bodily energy and thingly ineffability is Metzger's calling and his charge, an imperative to create abstract patterns out of the continuity script of bodies attempting to meet each other in time, to seize upon each other in the unexpectedly rhyming couplets of female-female and male-male.

Politically, the progressive aspirations and affects of *Score* signal a polymorphously perverse ideal of erotic play, embodied in the resonant line, uttered in different moments, with slightly different inflections, by both Jack and Elvira that "I'd climb aboard a porcupine if it struck my fancy." What better articulation of the erotic equanimity of the era? Marriage is conceived by the film as a structure that can be tolerated at best, a limiting architecture to be innovated through alternative intimacies. Dismantling the model of "two" and the hetero-centric couple form in the interest of more labile arrangements of kinship and pleasure, the film presumes that the modern couple so central to and so troubled in the art cinema is here divested of any aspiration towards social reproduction or productivity, and the desire of the married partners should only multiply and attract thirds and fourths. Each partner's sexual autonomy is preserved, as Eddie and Betsy accept each other's divergences, while a modified kinship arrangement—sexuality as sociality itself—is perpetuated. No wonder then that by the end of the film, Betsy and Eddie leave Elvira and Jack in the morning-after lurch, apt pupils who run off, joyously absconding with Mike the repairman on a new "score" of their own. While Jack and Elvira make do by planning to see a Michael Powell film, a waiter at a café suddenly magnetizes their attentions, and the cycle of seduction time begins again. The sing-song voiceover tells us in conclusion that "in the meantime, for there is always a meantime, fantasy reigns supreme." This designation of an erstwhile, an expectant time between, encapsulates both the historicity and the suspended pleasures of the 1970s erotic imagination, as well as Metzger's.

1.
Richard Brown, "Radley Metzger: Auteur of the Erotic," *Today's Filmmaker*, August 1971, 27–28.

2.
Vincent Canby, "Essy the Spirit, Essy the Body," *New York Times*, 26 May 1968.

3.
Addison Verrill, "Test for Right Sell to Wrong Sex," *Variety*, 3 July 1974, 17.

4.
Richard Corliss, *Village Voice*, 11 December 1969. Quoted in Museum of Modern Art film notes, *Camille 2000*, "New Acquisitions" screening, 22 April 1976, MoMA Film Study Center, New York.

5.
Stephen Gallagher, "The Libertine: On *Score*'s Radley Metzger" (interview), *Filmmaker*, Summer 1997, http://www.filmmakermagazine.com/archives/issues/summer1997/metzger.php (accessed 1 August 2013).

Film Stills

61
Nelson Lyon
The Telephone Book, 1971

62, 63
Dušan Makavejev
WR: Mysteries of the Organism, 1971

64
Vilgot Sjöman
I am Curious (Yellow), 1967

65
Roger Vadim
Barbarella, 1968

66, 67
Nagisa Oshima
In the Realm of the Senses, 1976

68, 69
Southeastern Pictures Corporation
Queens at Heart, 1967

70, 71
Lisa Crafts
Desire Pie, 1976

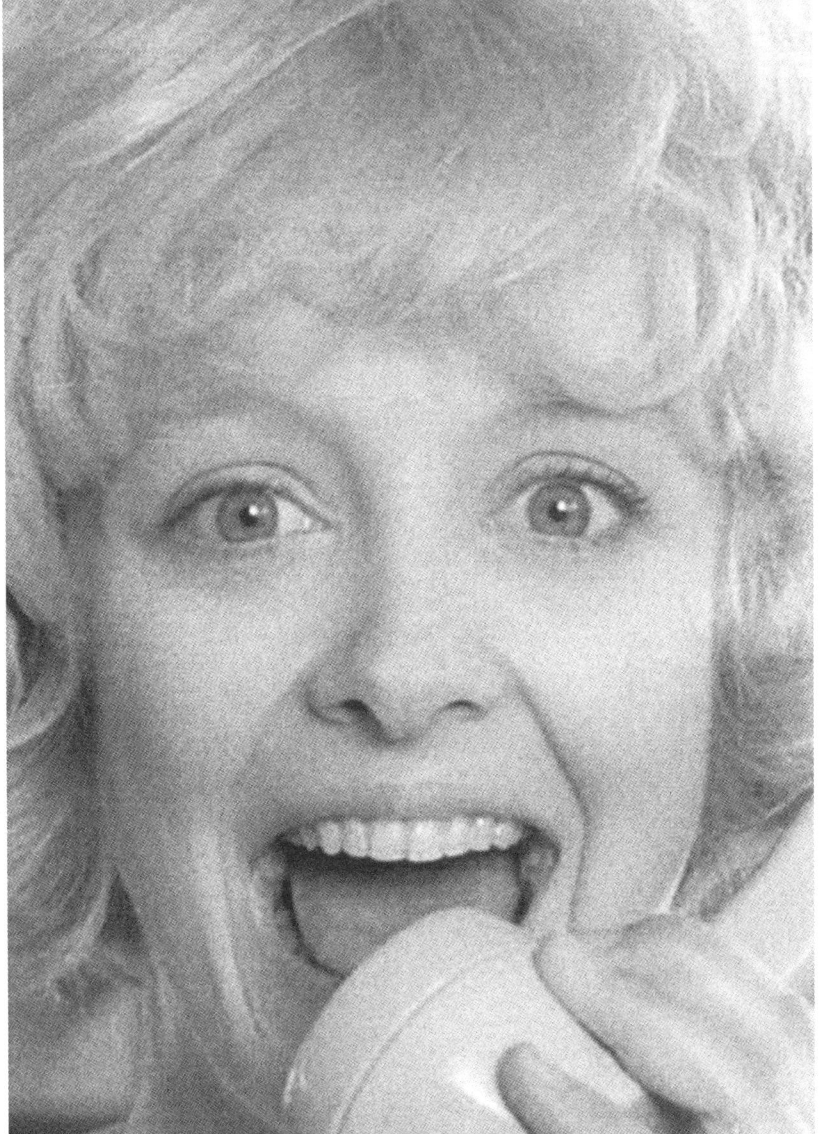

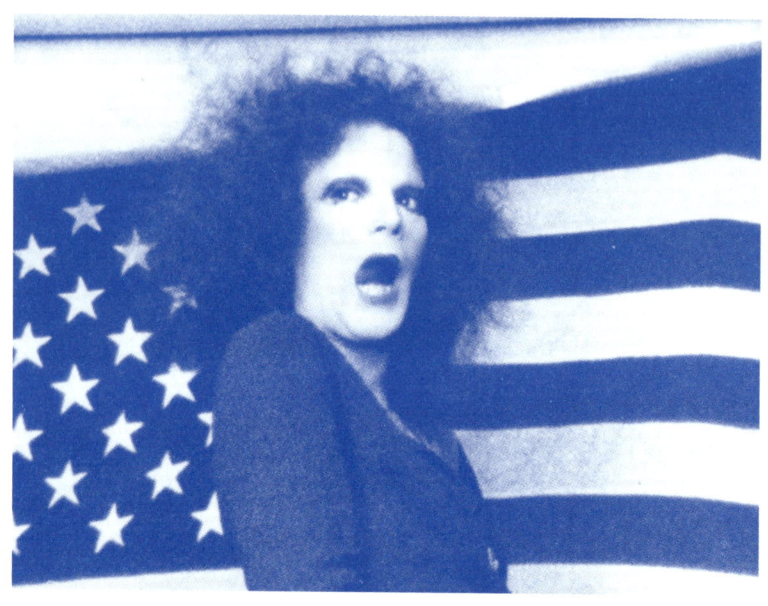

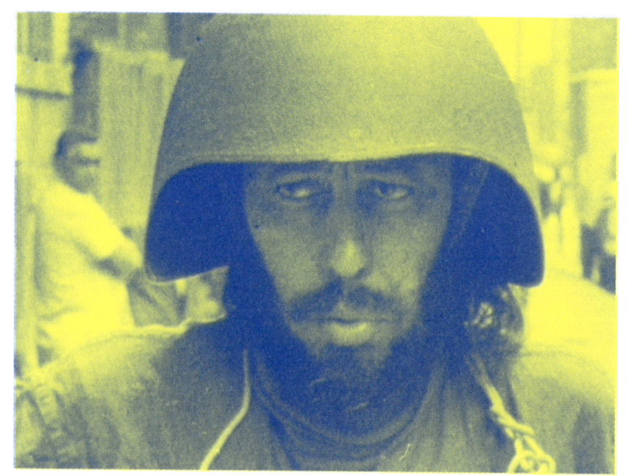

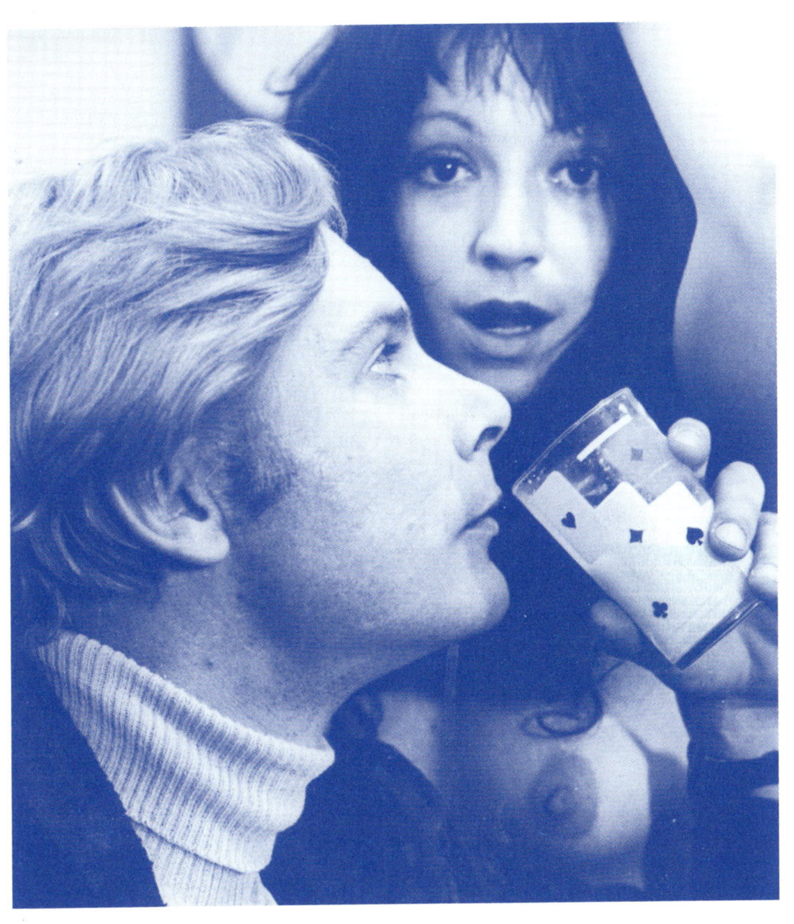

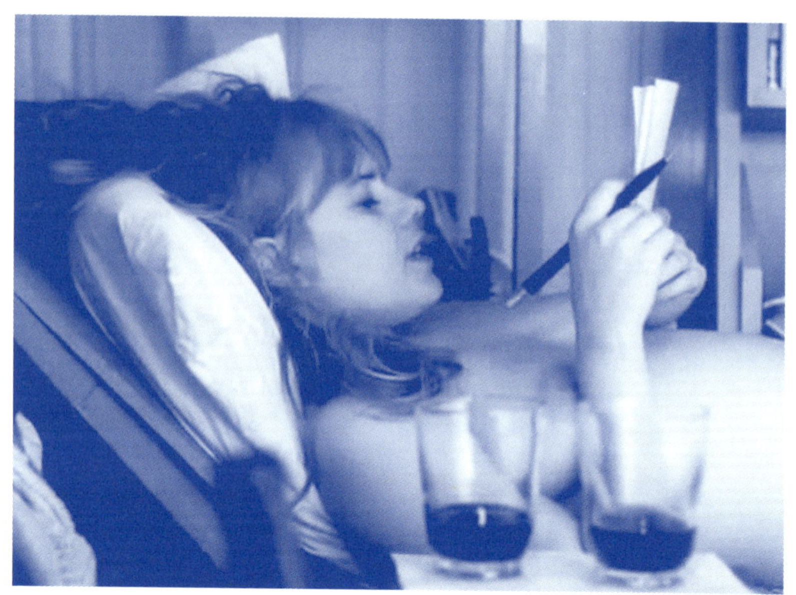

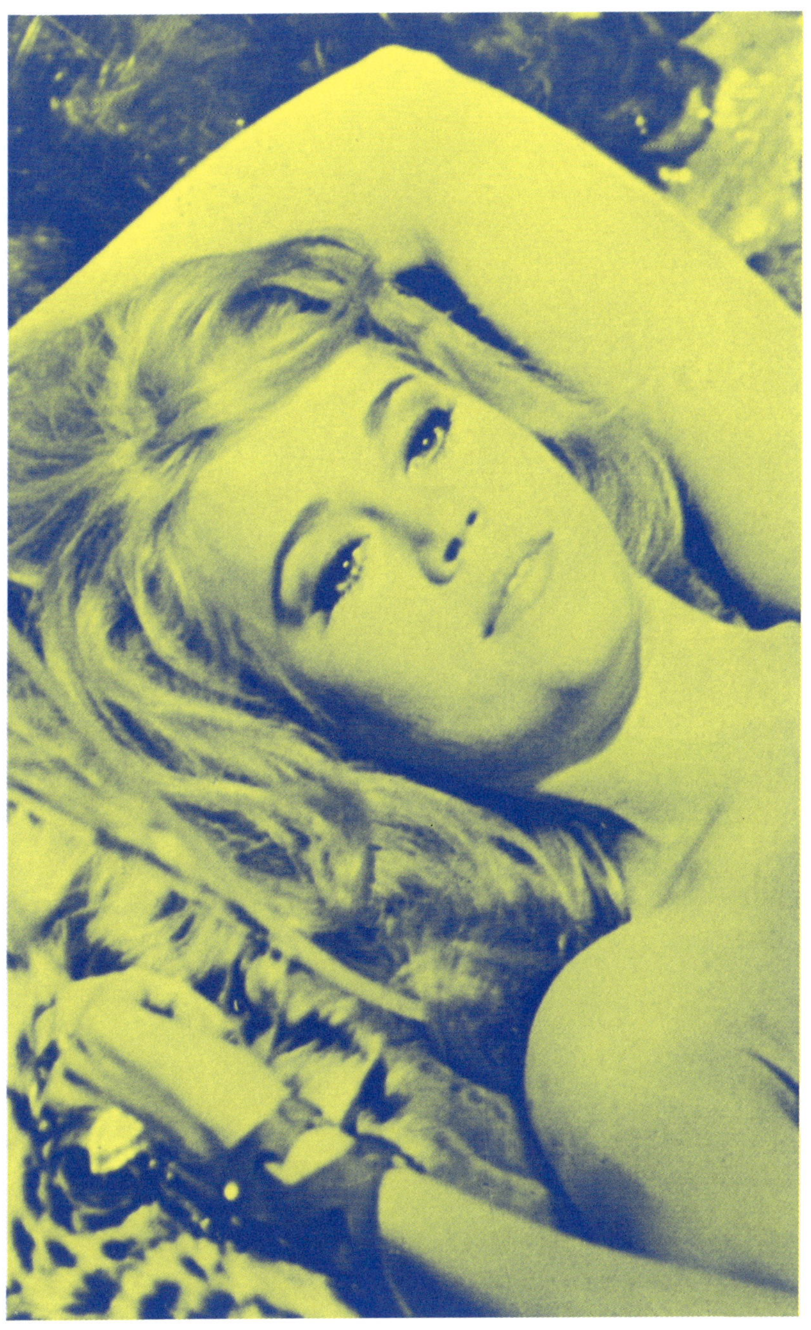

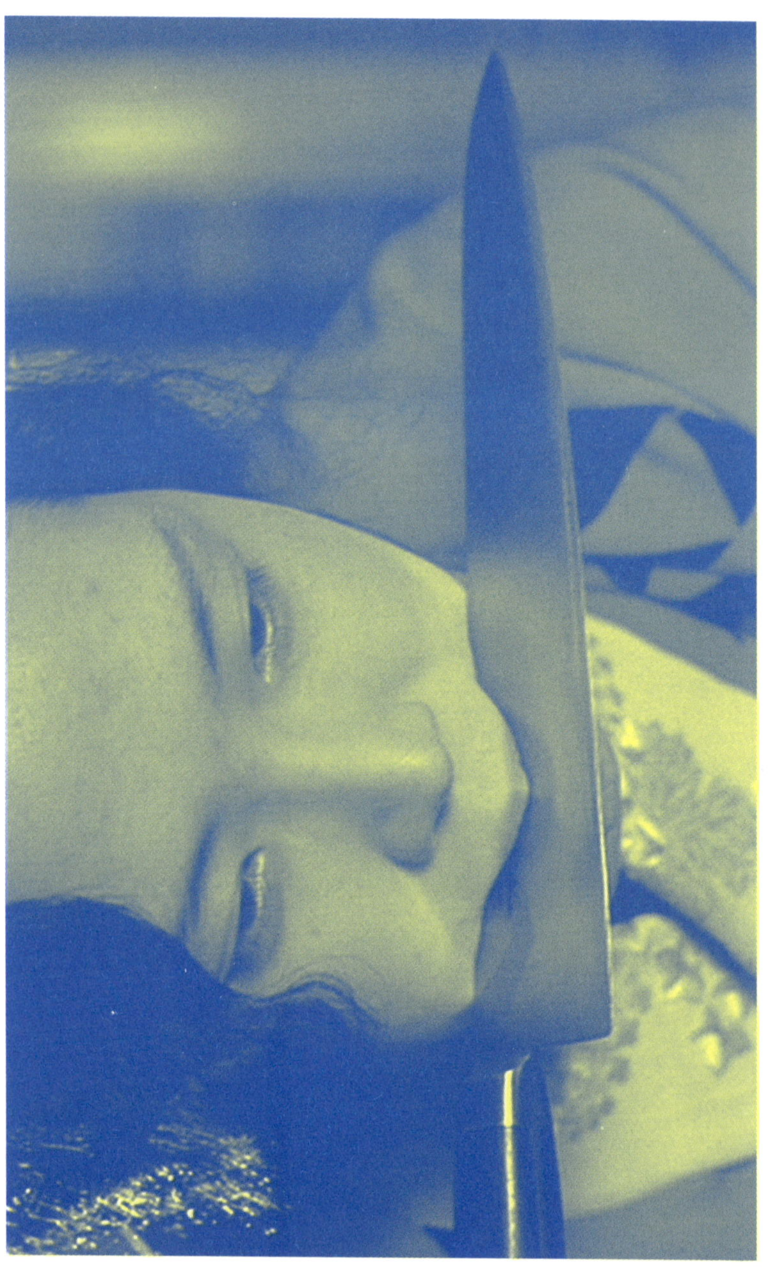

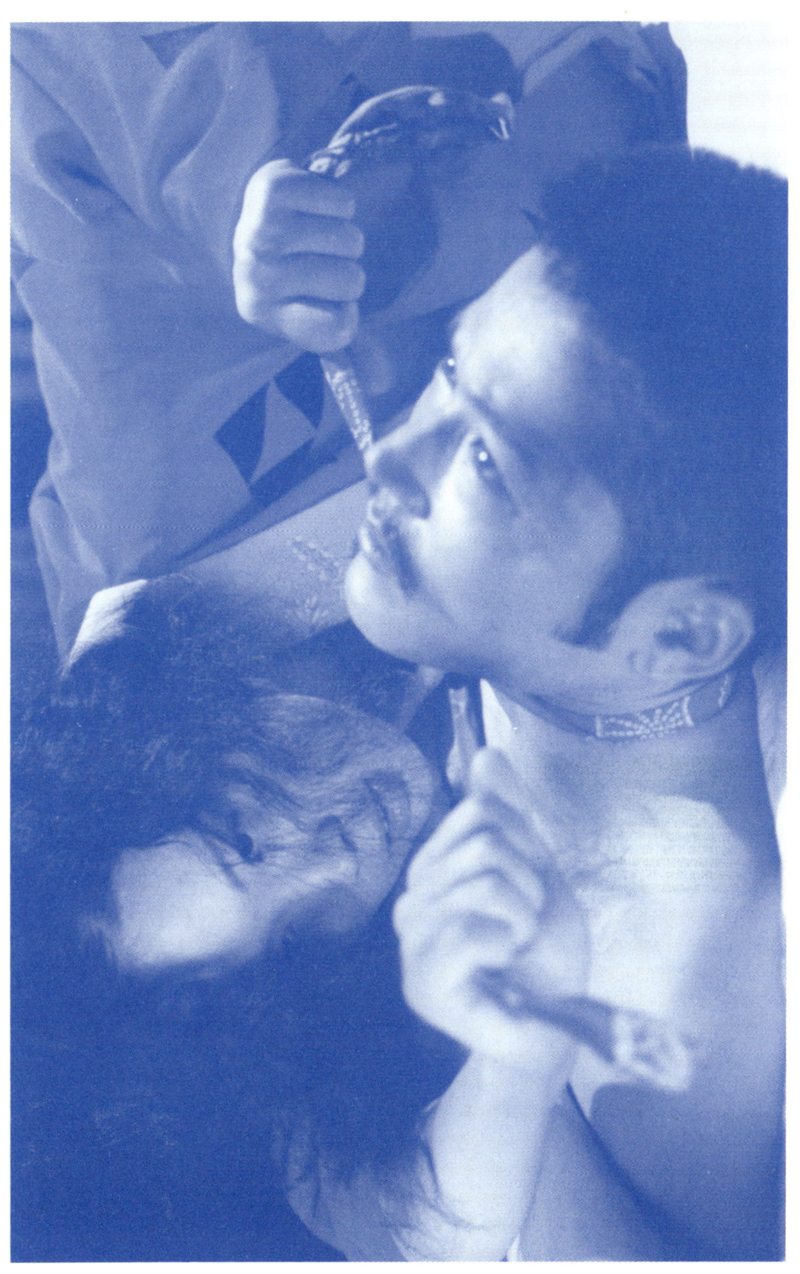

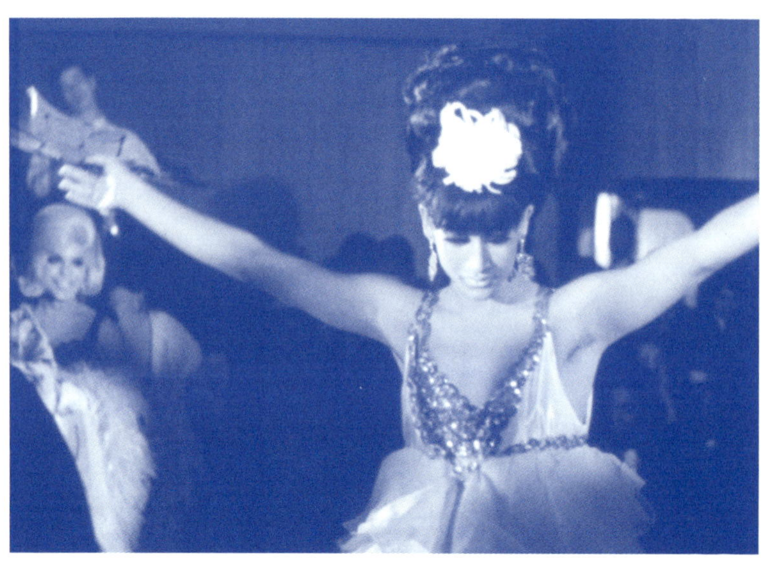

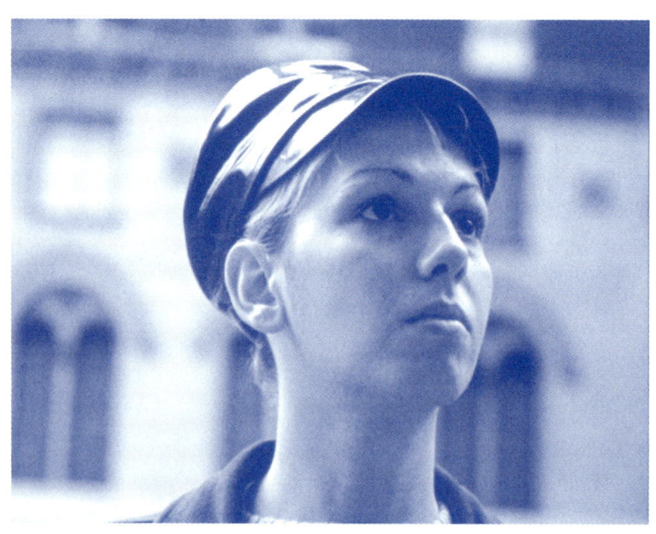

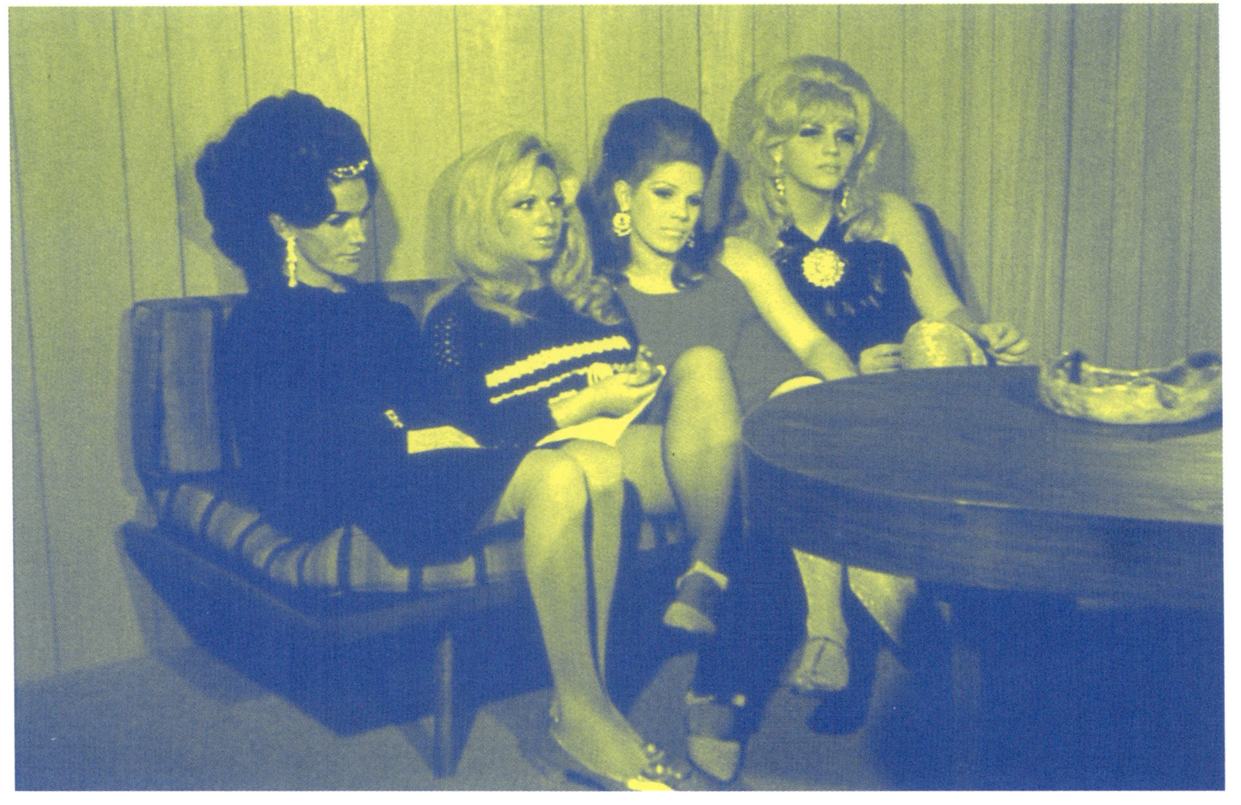

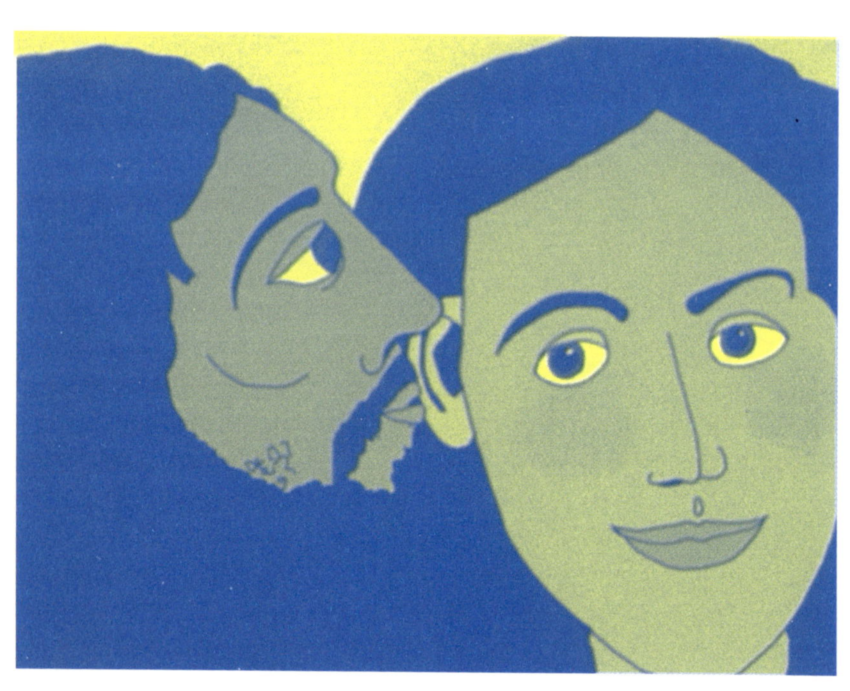

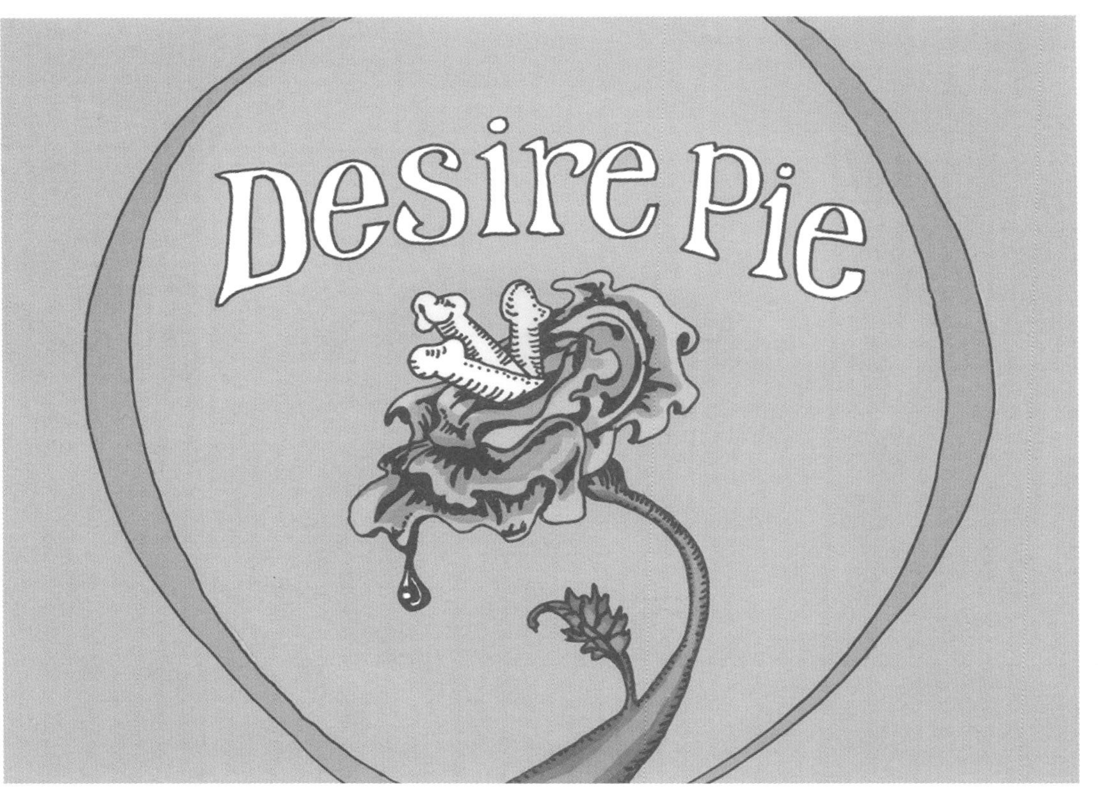

Desire Pie

Whitney Strub

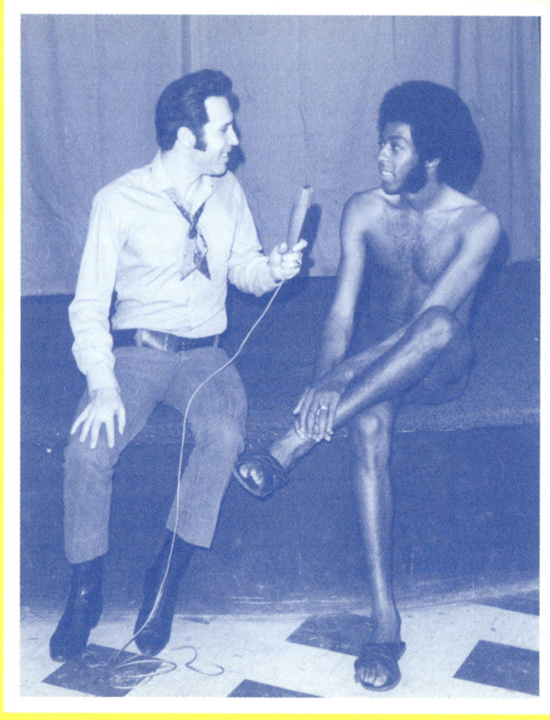

Rocco interviewing dancer Bob Philpot on the set of *Meat Market Arrest*, 1970

Hey Look Me Over: The Films of Pat Rocco

When Pat Rocco arrived at the Meat Market in early 1970, so too did the police. Rocco was at the gay nightclub (in El Segundo, near Los Angeles International Airport) to film a nude dance; the cops were there to harass patrons and arrest the owner. So Rocco simply shot the scene as it occurred: a plainclothes officer roaming the bar checking IDs, the owner being hauled out. It's easy to miss the profound importance of the resulting short, *Meat Market Arrest*; the whole event plays out with the quality of a weary routine, and the ever-affable, even-keeled Rocco narrates live and onscreen, no firebrand: "I think it's another example of what might be considered by some people, and I think I would venture to say certainly my own opinion, a form of police harassment."

In fact, Rocco had captured the daily texture of the homophobic police state that was the United States well into the 1970s, live on camera, in a way no other filmmaker had.[1] *Meat Market Arrest* is singular in its visual documentation of the casual terrorizing of queer people that was standard operating procedure for police around the nation. It doesn't look like terror, because most everyone involved is used to it; at the same time, this is a population criminalized simply on account of their identities. "The Whole World is Watching" was a popular New Left slogan of the time, often chanted against violent authorities—but even the ostensibly progressive New Left remained enmeshed in homophobic attitudes at the time. Rocco neither looks nor sounds like an angry radical, but even in 2013 it can be a courageous act to point a camera at a cop, so much the more so in a gay bar forty years ago. Because he did point and shoot, we have this unique filmic record.

If *Meat Market Arrest* nods toward Pat Rocco's importance as a gay documentarian, it doesn't end there. Three days later, he returned to the bar to finally capture the nude dance. In the film's second half, he chats with lawyer

Hey Look Me Over

Walter Culpepper and dancer Bob Philpot about the pending cases, then lets Philpot perform, a sweet, mellow, fully nude dance—to be shown to a judge, in fact, in an effort to establish the artistic merit of the Meat Market's dancers. Here we see Rocco's other side: the groundbreaking erotic filmmaker whose joyful celebrations of gay eros boldly appeared at the Park Theatre in downtown Los Angeles in the summer of 1968, a year before Stonewall, and reveled in nude men carousing, running, jumping, kissing, and cavorting, all at a time when homosexual activity remained illegal even in the state of California. In some ways, *Meat Market Arrest* is the key to Rocco's entire expansive oeuvre, linking his twin cinematic imperatives through its insistent documentation of gay life and celebration of gay desire, even in the face of attempted suppression.

Rocco was a pioneering figure in the cultural wing of the sexual revolution, but his work goes too little remembered today. He tends to pop up in cameo appearances in various gay histories, but his rich and varied film work has received far too little sustained attention.[2] Though on a technical level he was no cinematic virtuoso, between 1968 and 1976 Rocco built a truly remarkable body of work. His erotic shorts helped spearhead the zesty vitality of gay liberation (not to mention paving the way for such hardcore icons as Wakefield Poole and fellow Angeleno Fred Halsted)—which his documentaries in turn captured, in styles that ranged from the black-and-white cinema verité of *Sign of Protest* (1970), in which gay activists demand the removal of an ineptly misspelled "Fagots Keep Out" sign at Barney's Beanery in West Hollywood, to the colorfully playful *We Were There* (1976), which features naked gay men, lesbians, and elephants all triumphantly marching in Gay Pride Week.

Rocco was born Pasquale Vincent Serrapica in an extended Brooklyn Italian-American family in 1934. His family moved to Southern California during his childhood, and he took his stage name only later, as he navigated the entertainment industry. Rocco's personal papers, at the ONE National Gay and Lesbian Archives, chart his ambitious course: from singing devotional music in the mid-1950s, to a contract with Hal Roach Studios and a television gig on the *Tennessee Ernie Ford Show*; from a movie theater he ran in the Simi Valley in the early sixties, through directing plays at mid-decade. Through these experiences, he learned not only showmanship but also the internal structural operations of the industry—both of which would pay off later.[3]

Rocco never resided in what was labeled by the late 1960s "the closet." Sexually active as a teenager, he had been forced to finish high school through distance learning with a tutor after refusing to deny his homosexuality. When he saw an ad in 1967 calling for physique photographers, he gave it a shot; where predecessors such as Bob Mizer of *Physique Pictorial* had been forced to coat their homoerotic images in thin alibis of nonsexualized bodybuilding, Rocco's generation rejected such subterfuges (which were necessary in 1950s America, to be sure—even without openly admitting his magazine's gay erotic charge Mizer was repeatedly arrested). Clark Polak, the Philadelphia publisher of *Drum*, had begun defiantly publishing openly gay, full-frontal nude images in 1965, and was joined shortly after by enterprising firms like Minneapolis's DSI.[4] Rocco followed suit.

Rocco's photographs sold well, and on something of a whim he began bringing an 8mm film camera to his shoots. The timing could not have been better: a confluence of forces, including gay activism and its push for increased visibility, the rapidly diminishing scope of obscenity laws (historically disproportionately aimed at queer expression), the market demands of a gay consumer base, and the broader spirit of sexual revolution, all worked together to open a new space for gay erotic expression. He entered gay film history not as an activist, nor through the queer underground of Warhol, Anger, or Kuchar. ("I didn't know there was a gay avant-garde," he recalls today). Instead, he belongs to a history of gay entrepreneurship, which the historian David Johnson has recently argued played a formative role in modern gay politics.[5] Rocco capitalized on his own good looks, appearing shirtless with a camera in the catalogs for his Bizarre Productions—which also emphasized positivity, declaring, "we are especially proud of the movies offered here."[6]

Gay erotica long preceded 1968, of course—but as a private, underground, or black-market activity. Thanks to such archives as the Kinsey Institute, the GLBT Historical Society in San Francisco, and Cornell University's Human Sexuality Collection (among many others), not to mention two generations of historians too numerous to mention, we now have access to personal hardcore photograph collections dating back to the nineteenth century, handwritten and mimeographed smut stories passed around as samizdat literature in a homophobic society, and "physique" movies of barely-clad men posing, wrestling, and occasionally coming just to the brink of overtly romantic expressions. But when Pat Rocco's micro-budgeted films premiered at the Park Theater in the summer of 1968, billed as part of "the first homosexual film festival," they broke new ground.[7] So uncertain was the terrain that Rocco and the theater kept a lawyer on site, very conscious that arrests might interrupt the screening.

Formally and technically, Rocco's early films remained simple, focused primarily on naked male bodies. *Magic in the Raw* (1968) is paradigmatic: a five-minute short featuring a magician bringing into being a sexy cowboy, undressing him with each wave of a wand, then accidentally making his creation disappear with a misplaced tap. The jump cuts that remove each item of clothing are imported directly from the

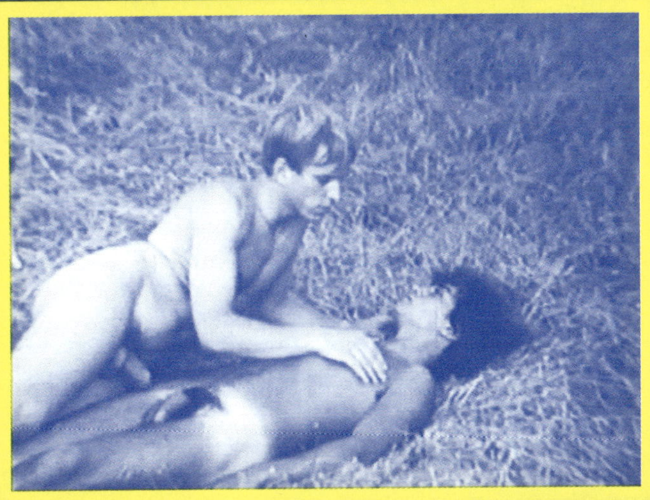

A Very Special Friend, 1968

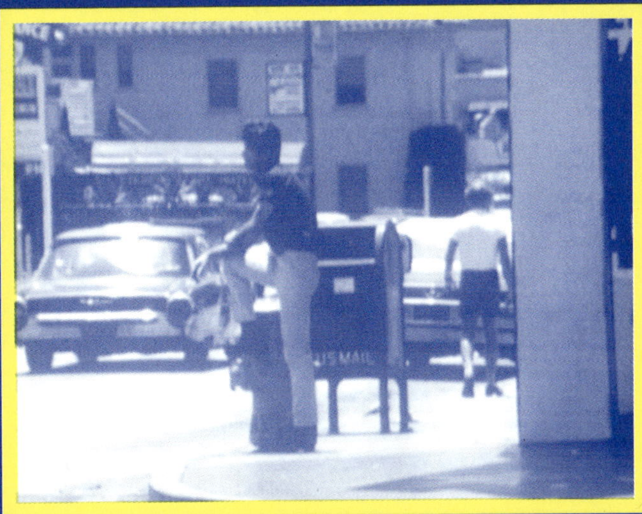

A Matter of Life, 1968

Hey Look Me Over

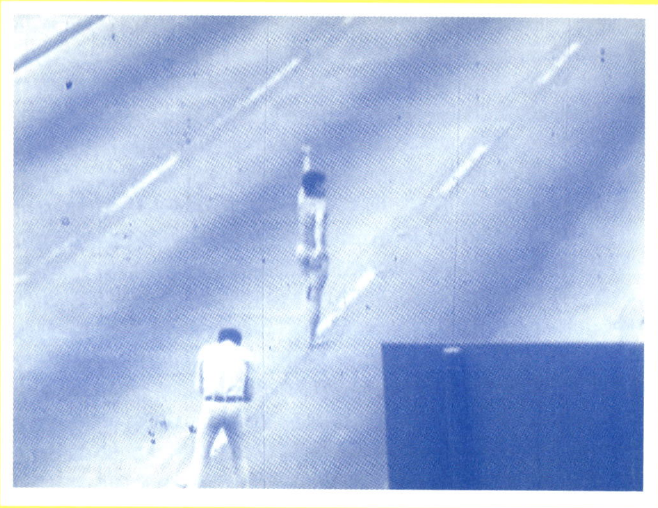

How to Shoot a Nude on the Freeway, 1969

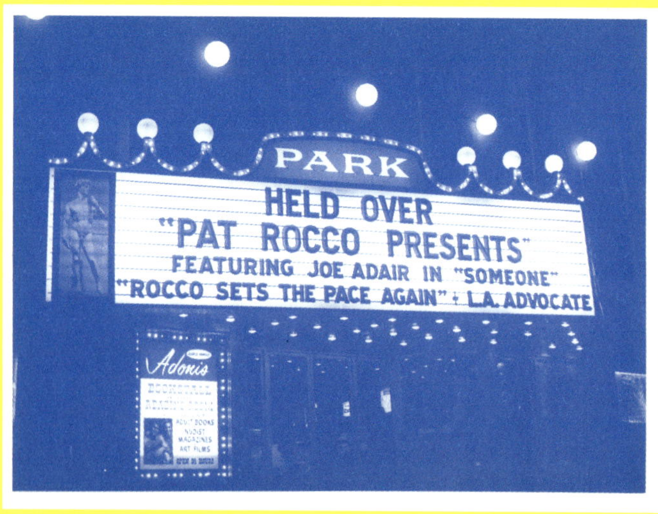

Park Theater, Los Angeles ca. 1969

1890s—indeed, other early shorts such as *Up, Up, and a-Wow* (1968), featuring four minutes of naked tree climbing—hark back to Eadweard Muybridge's early motion studies, while *The Gang That Couldn't Go Straight* (also 1968) utilizes silent slapstick humor in its chase scene that moves from foot to bike to pogo stick—naked, of course. But while the stylistic tropes looked backward, the playful, irreverent eroticism was very much a product of the late sixties, a bold gay self-assertion no less political for being funny and slightly clumsy.

Rocco showed experimental ambitions at times; *The Boy, the Forest, the Dream* (1968) begins with handwritten credits flashing in semi-psychedelic red, and after a pastoral striptease by Ted Huston among the streams and trails of Los Angeles National Forest's Mount Baldy, Rocco swerves to a jarring, Brakhagian dream sequence of pulsing, jerking camera moves and cuts. He flirted with darker existential themes at times, particularly in his films written by star Joe Adair, who plays an isolated, alienated hustler in *A Matter of Life* (1968) and Rocco's first feature-length narrative film, *Someone* (1968, again—truly an expansive body of work was generated this year alone!). The latter film shows how rapidly Rocco's ambitions expanded, and, though it's largely forgotten today, its bisexual ambivalence and unglamorous LA location shooting (more anticipatory of Jacques Demy's *Model Shop* or Antonioni's *Zabriskie Point* than reflective of, say, *Beach Blanket Bingo*) make it a fascinating historical relic. Rocco even won praise from *Variety*, which acknowledged his "sensitive filmmaking talent" with the style "of a romanticist, not a pornographer."[8]

His primary media base, however, was the gay press. From the start, Rocco's films won consistent adulation there, as typified by Jim Kepner's early 1969 rave review in the homophile magazine *Tangents*. Contrasting Rocco with the "awkward, backyard cock-danglers" of the "old physique photographers," not to mention "Anger's old pathologicals" and "Warhol's posturings," longtime activist and journalist Kepner saw in Rocco "something homosexuals had never before found on the screen:" "lyric and romantic depictions of male love and beauty, unmorbid and frankly physical, without the smirking leer." He found it "exhilarating, fresh, ideal, basic, and agonizingly beautiful."[9] As Rocco rolled out one successful set of shorts after another from 1968 to 1970, gay audiences clearly agreed. Success emboldened Rocco, and his films grew more adventurous on multiple fronts. While his initial shorts had featured abundant full-frontal male nudity, overt sexual content remained circumscribed by the threat of obscenity charges. Yet, already by the end of 1968, *A Very Special Friend* depicted two attractive young men cruising each other across Los Angeles, culminating in intense kissing and full-body naked contact as they rolled around Griffith Park. Though very much softcore, this was a step toward more graphic sexual content than publicly screened gay erotica had yet dared attempt—indeed, a 1969 set of shorts screened as "Pat Rocco Dares."

From the start, Rocco had employed courageous guerilla shooting, capturing remarkable footage of Hollywood Boulevard, Griffith Park, Echo Park, Los Feliz, and other hotspots of gay LA geography; above and beyond his significance as a gay filmmaker, he merits greater recognition as a Los Angeles filmmaker. For *A Breath of Love* (1969), he undertook the astonishing feat of filming a naked man (Brian Reynolds) dancing on the LA freeway. Rocco and friends blocked the heavily trafficked road by deliberately clogging it behind the shoot—as he then documented in the extraordinary *How to Shoot a Nude on the Freeway* (1969), which shows Rocco and crew returning for a second take after they forgot to shoot publicity photos. Entrepreneurial as always, Rocco called NBC, who showed up to tape the event—and

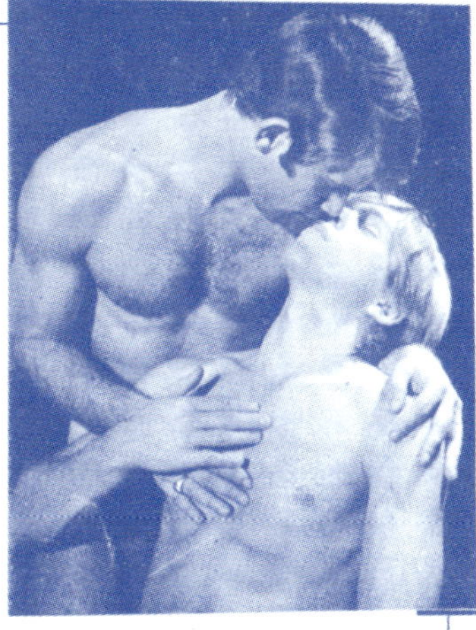

Advertisement for *Pat Rocco Dares*, 1969

also provide a protective cover of newsworthiness when the police arrived this time. In an equally risky venture, Rocco smuggled footage of two men cruising in *Disneyland for Disneyland Discovery* (1969)—which was promptly suppressed by corporate authorities, though it remains viewable at UCLA's Film & Television Archive, and represents one more thrilling assertion of gay presence in a distinctly heteronormative, "family" friendly setting.

Some of Rocco's earliest forays into documentary emanated naturally out of his erotic shorts. *Marco of Rio* (1969) documented a trip to Brazil, using sixteen-year-old tour guide Marco Antonio as a window onto local and tourist beefcake scenes, while that same year *The Groovy Guy* recorded a contest at a gay bar. Rocco's opening narration, typical of the personable, upbeat demeanor he had developed during his years in the entertainment industry, calls Los Angeles the "capital city of the west, with millions of happy people throughout," and as if to prove it, another 1969 short documentary, *A Man and His Dream*, highlights the Reverend Troy Perry, founder of the gay-oriented Metropolitan Community Church and a crucial figure in LGBT religious history. True to form, Rocco emphasizes the positive, downplaying the adversity Perry faced in favor of an idyllic vision of his life. All of the happiness might seem at a four-decade remove blithe or apolitical, but in contrast to the demeaning and insulting images perpetrated at the time by the mass media and bigoted authorities (including psychologists, who considered homosexuality pathological until 1973), its very pride and simplicity stood as stark rejoinder.

By 1970, however, a grittier and more explicitly oppositional politics began to appear in Rocco's nonfiction films. His omnibus Mondo Rocco that year combined both erotic shorts (such as *The Luckiest Cat in Town*, featuring naked men playing with the titular feline, quite charmingly) and his increasingly sophisticated documentaries, including the aforementioned *Meat Market Arrest*. *Homosexuals on the March* showed a rally for consenting-adults legislation that would decriminalize homosexual activity. It took another five years for California to pass it, but Rocco captured an emboldened, multiracial, multigenerational movement, whose activists sport interlocking arms and slogans like "Oral can be moral" and, from *Sign of Protest*, "Give me sex or give me death." Almost no other press showed up to cover the rally—or the subsequent motorcade down Hollywood Boulevard also included in the film, as gay activists sing "We Shall Overcome." In the middle of it, Rocco gets pulled over for standing in a car with his camera—and, naturally, keeps shooting.

If 1970 was a banner year for Rocco, 1971 was for the representations of gay life: the year hardcore broke. Wakefield Poole's *Boys in the Sand* opened in December of that year, with Fred Halsted's *L.A. Plays Itself* following a few months later, and Rocco's romantic visions would soon be displaced by the ethos of maximum graphic exposure, which he did not embrace. As hardcore prospered, he followed his muse, spending years and most of his personal savings on *Drifter* (also known as *Two-Way Drift*, completed in 1975), a feature-length film again written by and starring Joe Adair, reprising his favorite role as an ambivalent hustler. The film won positive commentary in outlets from *Gaytimes* to the *Hollywood Reporter*, but Rocco was unable to secure broader distribution, and it never received wide attention. Today a lost film to all but the archival researcher, *Drifter* deserves a belated release; its local scenery would make the better-funded New Hollywood location fetishists jealous.

After the next year's gay pride documentary *We Were There* (also an unsung and sadly noncirculating treasure that preserves the texture of gay life several years after

Hey Look Me Over

Stonewall and just before Anita Bryant's homophobic *Save Our Children* crusade ushered in the forty-year Republican assault on equality), Rocco turned to local gay politics in Los Angeles, ran an LGBT homeless shelter, and ultimately moved to Hawai'i, where he ran another movie theater and recorded more music, among other pursuits. His films continue to await a full rediscovery—even as they still demand, as his early short insisted, *Hey Look Me Over*.

1.
The closest comparison might be William E. Jones's *Tearoom* (2007), which recovers police-surveillance footage of restroom cruising in 1960s Mansfield, Ohio.

2.
See Thomas Waugh, *Hard to Imagine: Gay Male Eroticism in Photography and Film before Stonewall* (New York: Columbia University Press, 1996), 270; Jeffrey Escoffier, *Bigger Than Life: The History of Gay Porn Cinema from Beefcake to Hardcore* (Philadelphia: Running Dog Press, 2009), 50–57; John Burger, *One-Handed Histories: The Eroto-Politics of Gay Male Video Pornography* (New York: Harrington Park Press, 1995), 14; Richard Dyer, *Now You See It: Studies in Lesbian and Gay Film* (New York: Routledge, 1990); David James, *The Most Typical Avant-Garde: History and Geography of Minor Cinemas in Los Angeles* (Berkeley, CA: University of California Press, 2005), 371–72. Efforts to recuperate Rocco include Whitney Strub, "Mondo Rocco: Mapping Gay Los Angeles Sexual Geography in the Late-1960s Films of Pat Rocco." *Radical History Review 2012*, no. 113 (2012): 13–34; and Brian Wuest, "Defining Homosexual Love Stories: Reconsidering the History of Pat Rocco's All-Male Films at the Park Theatre," (2012) at http://www.cinema.ucla.edu/sites/default/files/Wuest_ARSC2012.pdf (accessed 17 August 2103).

3.
Rocco biographical material based on: Contract with Hal Roach Studios, 16 April 1956, box 1, folder 1, Pat Rocco Papers, ONE National Gay & Lesbian Archives,

Los Angeles (hereafter Rocco Papers); Park Theatre Special Notice, January 1961, box 17, folder 8, Rocco Papers; see also Rocco Papers finding aid (http://www.oac.cdlib.org/findaid/ark:/13030/kt3k4025zg/ (accessed 15 August 2013); Paul Siebenand, "The Beginnings of Gay Cinema in Los Angeles: The Industry and Its Audience" (PhD diss., University of Southern California, Los Angeles, 1975); Rocco interview with Jim Kepner, 27 April 1983 (video at UCLA Film & Television Archive, transcript at http://www.cinema.ucla.edu/sites/default/files/Rocco.pdf (accessed 1 August 2013); author's discussions with Pat Rocco, February 2011 and August 2013.

4.

On Polak, see Marc Stein, *City of Sisterly and Brotherly Loves: Lesbian and Gay Philadelphia, 1945–1972* (Philadelphia: Temple University Press, 2004).

5.

David Johnson, "Physique Pioneers: The Politics of 1960s Gay Consumer Culture," Journal of Social History 43, no. 4 (2010): 867–92.

6.

Bizarre Productions, Catalog #25 (1969), box 4, folder 1, Rocco Papers.

7.

Park Theatre flyer, summer 1968, box 5, folder 8, Rocco Papers.

8.

[Somebody review,] *Variety*, clipping, box 6, folder 5, Rocco Papers.

9.

Jim Kepner, "The Films of Pat Rocco," *Tangents*, February/April 1969, 27–30.

Herb Shellenberger

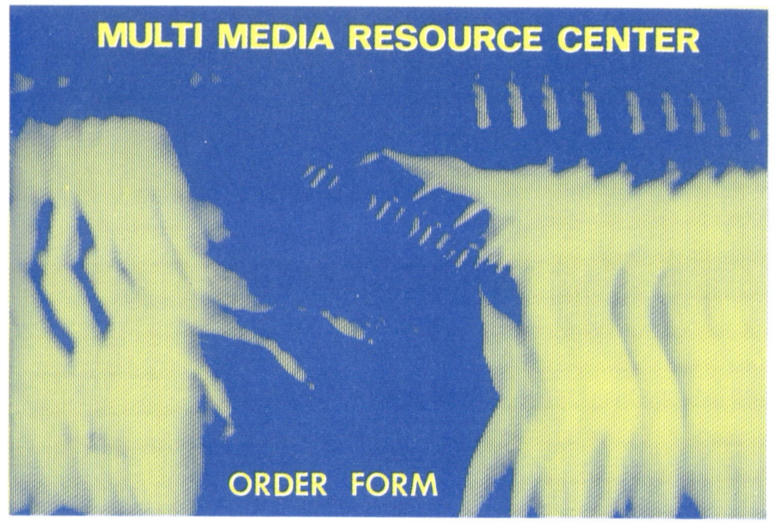

All images *Multi-Media Resource Center Catalog, 1974*

Radical Sex Education Films & San Francisco's Multi-Media Resource Center

The sexual revolution can be interpreted as a pervasive force in the global consciousness of the 1960s and 1970s. *Free to Love: The Cinema of the Sexual Revolution* considers a variety of films from that era that portray, challenge, and break attitudes about sex and sexuality. But beyond the cinema there was another important use of moving images relating to sexuality: films with the purpose of sex education, sex instruction, and sex therapy. While there were likely thousands of films produced and distributed to schools, churches, community groups, and prisons (among other institutions), the films made and circulated by San Francisco's Multi-Media Resource Center (MMRC) stand out as a particular and resonant group when considering the impact of moving images during the sexual revolution. These films, made available for the purposes of education and therapy, reflect the liberalizing of sexual attitudes as well as the need for sexual self-discovery of and empathy for those of different sexual preferences. Furthermore, the MMRC brought together a diverse array of films (those they produced and those they licensed from other filmmakers), and in doing so created a cohesive body of films on clinical sexual health alongside films that would be considered by many standards avant-garde, experimental, or underground.

History of the MMRC

The Multi-Media Resource Center grew out of the National Sex Forum (NSF), an organization that was organized initally by the Glide Methodist Church in the 1960s. The founders of the NSF and MMRC, Ted McIlvenna and Laird Sutton, believed sexuality was their ministry and that a vital part of their outreach would be done through the creation and distribution of films.[1] The MMRC provided sale and rental of films and videos to schools, churches, social agencies, colleges and universities, and "professional persons engaged in education, research, counseling and therapy."[2] These films were not available for theatrical engagements, but were limited to screenings by educational groups or for use in library collections. Unlike clinical or scientific sexologists, McIlvenna and Sutton stressed a humanistic approach to sexology.[3] They strove to help people understand and embrace their own sexual feelings, and examined the wide spectrum of human sexuality and its varying impacts on individuals. With these goals, the MMRC produced and distributed films focused on a wide variety of topics: heterosexuality, homosexuality, lesbianism, bisexuality, group sex, masturbation and male/female genitalia, gender identity, birth and birth control, massage, and disability, among others. Films placed emphasis on letting subjects tell their stories or demonstrate their sexual activities, rather than prescribing narrated feelings and placing strictures on them.

It is important that the organization acted as both the producer (through the NSF) and a distributor of films. Sometimes the distinction between a film produced by the NSF and one by an outside filmmaker/producer is more obvious than others.[4] Among the non-NSF films, some were clearly produced from clinical or educational perspectives on sexual issues, but there were also many films made by independent filmmakers with experimental, avant-garde, and underground-cinema aspirations. These films were removed from their original contexts and recategorized as films for sex education and therapy. Rarely are experimental films ascribed any sort of utilitarian function, so the act of reassigning films that at best were only tangentially created with any type of sex education or therapy purpose was a move that required considerable creativity.

RICH & JUDY

FILMMAKER: Laird Sutton. MUSIC: Larry Vogt. PRODUCTION CONSULTANT: Ted McIlvenna. PRODUCER: Multi Media Resource Center, 1971. CATEGORY: Heterosexuality.

COLOR . . . . **12 minutes**
SOUNDTRACK; guitar composition

SUBJECT:

This film is a sunny and affectionate picture of two young people very much in love. They have been married several years and really enjoy each other.

The films begins with them riding motor bikes on a country road. Beside the road, they take delight in her body. They then are seen by a swimming pool.

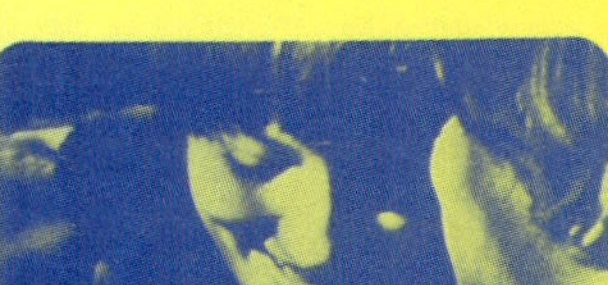

Judy revels in Rich's undressing her, and begins fellatio. They each rub some body oil on the other. In a brief scene, Judy is having oral sex with Rich, above her, while she rocks her pelvis in excitement and pleasure. Her sex flush is visible. In intercourse, Rich is on top and Judy rests her legs on his shoulders. She has a striking orgasm, with much motion. After a rest, they continue to pleasure each other, and enjoy the swimming pool.

SUGGESTED USE:

This film is popular as the one film to use, and especially as the one heterosexual film. It is a gentle, introductory film.

16mm.   Rental: $30.00/Sale: $175.00
S-8mm.   Sale: $100.00

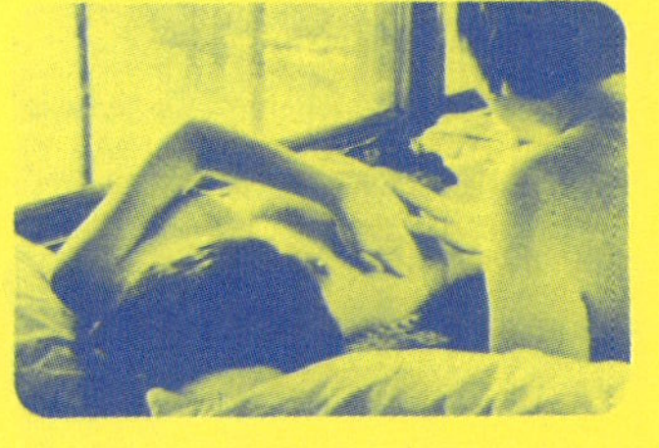

FULLNESS

FILMMAKER: Laird Sutton. FILMING ASSISTANCE: Salli Rasberry. PRODUCTION ASSISTANT: Bob Durham. PRODUCTION CONSULTANT: Ted McIlvenna. TITLES: Linda Cox. THANKS TO: Department of Human Sexuality at the University of Minnesota Medical School, Richard A. Chilgren, M.D., Director.

COLOR . . . . **13 minutes.**
SOUNDTRACK: music.

SUBJECT:

A young couple share their relationship and sexuality, while she is 8 months pregnant. The two are seen in several settings and with their first child. A feeling of peace and wholeness pervades the film.

They flow easily from lying together into sexual activity. She leisurely performs fellatio and he manipulates her genitals, all in a caring atmosphere of gentleness. Later, they have intercourse, in two positions.

In the final scene, they continue touching and light, playful massage.

SUGGESTED USE:

Particularly for couples in pregnancy, this film shows some of the possibilities of sexual activity available to them. FULLNESS is excellent for sex education classes and programs.

16mm.   Rental: $30.00/Sale: $175.00

Shellenberger

Radical Sex Education

UNFOLDING

FILMMAKER: Constance Beeson. CONSUL-
TANT: Laird Sutton. PRODUCER: National
Sex Forum, 1969. CATEGORY: Hetero-
sexuality. CROSS REFERENCE: Erotic Fan-
tasy.
BLACK AND WHITE . . . . **17 minutes.**
SOUNDTRACK: music.

SUBJECT:

Through a series of dream-like episodes, UNFOLDING suggests universal
awareness—aloneness, fantasies, search-
ing, touching, loving.

In the vague suggestion of a story,
nature and sea mix with hints of legend,
ritual, and poetry. UNFOLDING becomes one's own folklore of imaginings.
Double and triple exposure blend ocean,
hills, sun, woman, and man, to portray
subterranean feelings, ethereal feelings,
the freeing of self, in loving and lovemaking, culminating in orgasm.

While various persons take part in the
film fantasy, two couples are focused
on. One very young couple move
through myth to find and enjoy one
another. The other, a bearded man in
his thirties and a young woman, take
viewers with them to pleasure and orgasm. Original music composition.

SUGGESTED USE:

It is suitable both as a warm introductory film and as a fine closing statement. It was the first film commissioned
by the National Sex Forum, and has
been used with persons as young as high
school age, in a variety of groups seeking to deal with feelings and values
about sexuality. Its richness of imagery
makes it useable alone, or in combina-
tion with other material.

16mm. Rental: $35.00/Sale: $200.00
S-8mm. Sale: $100.00

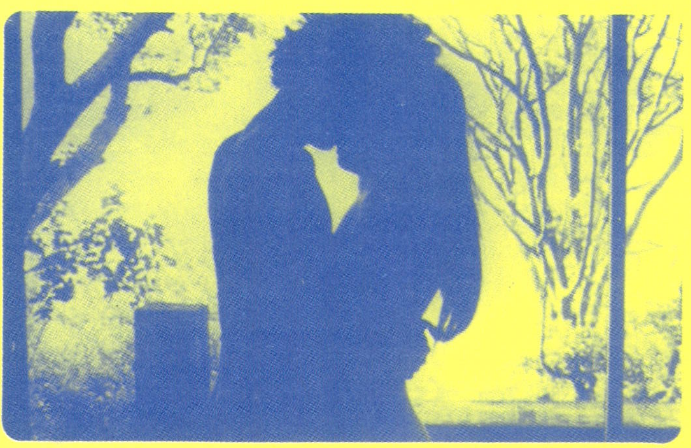

Shellenberger

The 1974 MMRC catalog introduced its two *auteur* sex filmmakers, Constance Beeson and Laird Sutton. Beeson and Sutton were the filmmakers with the most films available from MMRC, and as the Center's media director Sutton was the more prolific of the two. The catalog describes both filmmakers' philosophies towards filming, listing such details as the type of film stock they preferred. The films produced by Beeson and Sutton were referred to as "pattern films," films that in general showed the pattern of a single person, couple, or group engaged in sexual activity, beginning with the subject prior to the act of sexual stimulation, through climax and resolution.

Rich and Judy (Laird Sutton, 1970), a typical pattern film, begins with folk guitar and the eponymous couple riding through a wooded area on a motorbike. We see multiple exposures showing layered images as well as shots slipping in and out of focus. The look is aesthetically similar to the work of independent filmmakers from the era such as Jonas Mekas or Gregory Markopoulos. The couple begins kissing and caressing. They move to an outdoor deck and begin playfully undressing and engaging in sexual acts. As their activities progress, the music becomes more intense, with electric guitars punctuated by tremolo. There are close-ups showing penetration and the film is filled in general with flourishes of adventurous cinematography. A number of Sutton's films share this general structure, such as *Free* (1971, showing a black heterosexual couple), *Vir Amat* (1971, with a male homosexual couple), *Fullness* (1974, showing a heterosexual couple with a pregnant woman), and *A Ripple in Time* (1974, with an older heterosexual couple). Other films are less conventional, like *View From the Top* (1972), a three-minute film that shows a close-up of an uncircumcised penis during masturbation. Raga music plays on its soundtrack and there are traces of rapid, flicker-film-style editing. Following a violent orgasm (with sound effects), the film quickly ends.

Noted film critic and founder of Cinema 16 Amos Vogel expounded on the aesthetic joys of the MMRC films in his Independents column in the May/June 1982 issue of *Film Comment*. He describes Laird Sutton's *Sun Children*: "A young couple, at a secluded, sun-lit beach, undress, engage in mutual oral sex, then intercourse and orgasm, all visible. Despite its 'romantic' overlay of location and sound (bird cries and waves), it is a more accurate example of erotic realism than *I Am Curious (Yellow)*, which failed to display actual copulation. Some day—one hopes—the new Bertoluccis, De Niros, and Diane Keatons will be as honest in 70mm color and Dolby sound."[5] Vogel, an advocate for *film as a subversive art*, saw the MMRC films as honestly portraying sexual acts that both Hollywood and independent films often stopped short of, only implying these acts out of a sense of decorum or prudishness.

Not all reviews were so positive, though. The 1974 *Women's Film Coop Catalog* lists the films as a group in their recommendation of films not to see. The catalog explains, "out of the six films we've seen, five of them took place in an idealized setting (by the sea, in the unspoiled woods, etc.). All heterosexual love making was in the missionary position, the man on top at all times—and frankly, in a few films, it was doubtful how much the woman was getting out of the experience … The exploration of sexuality is important, but it must be done in a context of reality… as well as in contexts of mutual development, caring and sharing with each other."[6] The catalog goes on to urge the reader to avoid the films and "make [their] own home movies." While the critique the Women's Film Co-op raises is valid, it's hard to judge the films wholesale while seeing only a few, as there is such a variety among titles. And in the years following 1974, many more films were produced and/or distributed by the MMRC that spoke to female sexuality.

Distribution of films

In addition to the films produced in-house by the NSF, the MMRC distributed films that they licensed from other sources, including universities, production companies, and, most importantly, independent filmmakers themselves. When paging through the MMRC catalogs, one notices films made by experimental filmmakers like Barbara Hammer (*Dyketactics*, 1974), Jerry Abrams (*Eyetoon*, 1968), Scott Bartlett (*Lovemaking*, 1970), Gunvor Nelson (*Kirsa Nicholina*, 1969), and Anne Severson (now Alice Anne Parker, *Near the Big Chakra*, 1972, and *Riverbody*, 1970). Four films by James Broughton were also distributed: *The Bed* (1968), *Erogeny* (1976), *Hermes Bird* (1977), and *Song of the Godbody* (1977),[7] as were a number of films by lesser-known filmmakers such as Dirk Kortz, Lisa Crafts, Jan Oxenberg, Karen Johnson, and Michael Wallin. All these films were created by artist-filmmakers who did not make them with the original intention of their being used as tools for sex education or therapy. However, the MMRC kept an eye out for a broad spectrum of films that dealt with sexuality to include in their repertoire.

Many of these films appear in the MMRC catalogs under the heading "Erotic Fantasy," denoting those that portrayed abstract sexual situations intended to stimulate thought and discussion about the viewers' sexual fantasies. Others are listed under the heading "Humor and Mood Alteration," films meant to lighten the mood before, after, or in the middle of a program filled with a number of serious or weighty films. One such film was *Love Toad* (1971) by Greg Von Buchau. A short, playful, psychedelic stop-motion film, *Love Toad* shows two beanbag toads placed in a variety of

Radical Sex Education

adventurous positions, their sexual gymnastics soundtracked by Serge Gainsbourg and Jane Birkin's steamy 1967 *chanson* "Je t'aime … moi non plus." The 1974 MMRC catalog notes the suggested use for the film: "To open a program on sexuality, to change the pace or to relieve tension."[8]

Greg Von Buchau, who made the film as a student at San Francisco State University, screened *Love Toad* in the university's Film Finals competition to an audience of 650. After the program, the MMRC approached him "saying they wanted to market my movie as a mood lightener when they showed their sex education movies, [which] were pretty heavy."[9] The film was then added to the MMRC's distribution catalog, with the filmmaker and distributor splitting evenly the royalties from sales and rentals of 16mm prints. Buchau was issued a quarterly check for royalties, which added up to an amount of $90,000 over ten years, amazing considering that the student film was made for a cost of $75.[10] Had the film simply been distributed as an art film it would never have had the potential to become such a high earner. For the MMRC to place such artist-made films into a context (sex education and therapy) so different from that of their original intention was a radical act. While some experimental films may have been used, for example, as case studies of film technique, rarely have they ever been so greatly transformed by being placed in a different context.

Orphaned works?

Sadly, many of the films produced and distributed by the MMRC are not widely accessible today. It is possible to locate select MMRC-produced films in university libraries,[11] but many libraries have deaccessioned their 16mm collections as video and digital formats have become standard. The NSF and MMRC were eventually incorporated under the Institute for the Advanced Study of Human Sexuality, an

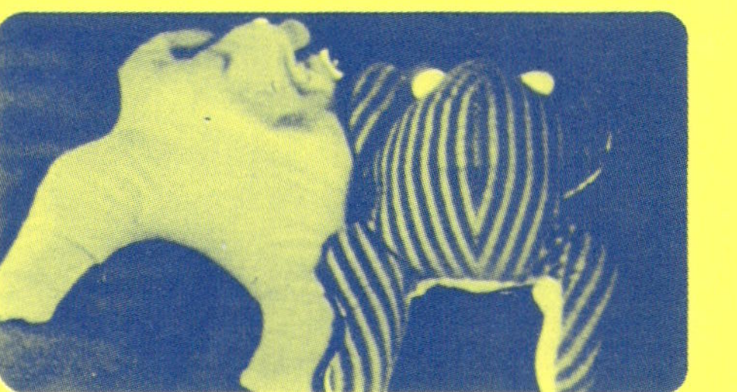

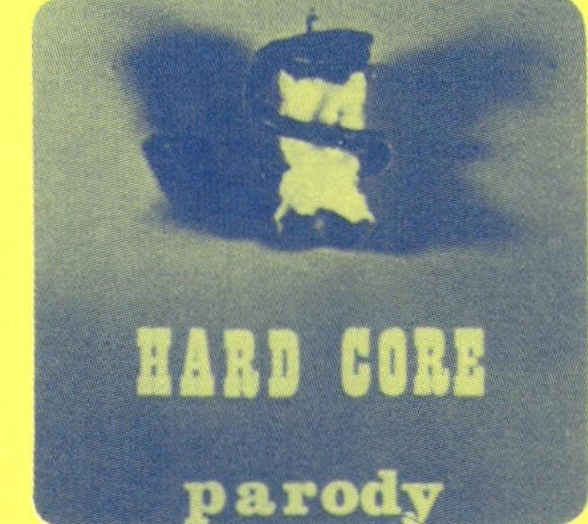

LOVE TOAD

FILMMAKER: Greg von Buchau, 1971. CATEGORY: Humor and Mood Alteration. **COLOR . . . . 2 minutes, 30 seconds. SOUNDTRACK: Music and Voices.**

SUBJECT:

A wonderfully funny film, Love Toad brings laughter to sex. Two colorful frog beanbags, with the help of the camera, engage in animated sexual activity. It is unforgettable, and always good for a smile.

"Love Toad, showing two beanbag frogs mating, is as deft and perky as it can be," **Howard Thompson** (New York Times).

SUGGESTED USE:

Use to open a program on sexuality, to change the pace, or to relieve tension.

16mm. Rental: $10.00/Sale: $50.00
S-8mm. Sale $50.00

JUMP CUT

FILMMAKER: Christine Pihl. PRODUCER: A C.R.-Auteur Production, 1962. SPECIAL THANKS TO: Richard Harkness. CATEGORY: Humor and Mood Alteration. **COLOR . . . . 1 minute, 30 seconds. SOUNDTRACK: Music and Narration.**

SUBJECT:

Our newest humor film, JUMP CUT, does an adult take-off on the story of "Goldilocks." A woman's pelvis is shown as she experiments with vegetables and other things, while a child's voice comments "too big," "too little," etc. Finally a man appears, and it's "just right!"

Very funny!
SUGGESTED USE:

An excellent film to begin a program of explicit material, it is also good slipped in between longer, more serious films.

16mm. Rental: $8.50/Sale: $40.00

Radical Sex Education

unaccredited, for-profit degree-granting institution that has offered programs of study and research in the field of human sexuality since the 1970s.[12] While the Institute has a library and archive that lists 300,000 films among its holdings, it is unclear what organizational standards and access policies exist for their use by researchers and the public.. The films that were licensed by the MMRC and produced by independent filmmakers fare better in general, with films by Barbara Hammer, James Broughton, Scott Bartlett, Alice Ann Parker (Anne Severson), and Lisa Crafts being readily available from the Film-Makers Cooperative, Canyon Cinema, or the filmmaker him- or herself. A number of Constance Beeson's 16mm films (woefully underrepresented in the remaining university holdings), including those produced by the NSF, were deposited with Canyon Cinema for rental after the filmmaker's death. While its for-profit status may prevent it from receiving preservation grants and contributions, one can hope that the Institute for the Advanced Study of Human Sexuality (perhaps with assistance from a nonprofit moving-image archive) can find a way to preserve and restore the films produced by the National Sex Forum and distributed by the Multi-Media Resource Center, as these films provide great insight into the attitudes, aesthetics, and techniques of sex education during the sexual revolution.

1.

A flurry of name changes occurred over the years, but the National Sex Forum was most often referred to as producer of the films, whereas the Multi-Media Resource Center was generally identified as the distributor. Alternate producer and distributor names include the National Sex and Drug Forum, The Exodus Trust, and Multi-Focus Inc.

2.

Multi-Media Resource Center Catalog, 1974, 2.

3.
Eithne Johnson, "The 'Sexarama': Or Sex Education as an Environmental Multimedia Experience," in *Sex Scene: Media and the Sexual Revolution*, ed. Eric Schaefer (Durham: Duke University Press, 2014), 332. Thank you to Eithne Johnson and Eric Schaefer for sharing an early version of this essay that discusses the National Sex Forum in the context of the "SAR" (Sexual Attitude Readjustment/Reassessment), a term that stood for both their theoretical approach to sex education as well as their technique of immersive presentations of audiovisual media.

4.
In the 1980-81 *Multi-Media Resource Center Catalog*, 64 of the listed films were produced by the NSF, whereas 83 were produced by an outside filmmaker or organization.

5.
Amos Vogel, "Missionary Positions," *Film Comment* (May/June 1982), http://www.filmcomment.com/article/missionary-positions/ (accessed October 5, 2013).

6.
Women's Film Coop Catalog, (San Francisco: The Mother Jones Press, c. 1975), 24.

7.
Broughton was also the subject of Laird Sutton's *James* (1979) in which he was erotically bathed and massaged.

8.
Multi-Media Resource Center Catalog, 1974, 43.

9.
Greg Von Buchau, email to author, 19 June 2013.

10.
Greg Von Buchau, email to author, 19 June 2013.

11.
Thank you to the University of Delaware Library Film and Video Collection Department and the staff at the Medgar Evers College Library for providing me access to film and video copies.

12.
"Mission," Institute for the Advanced Study of Human Sexuality, http://www.humansexualityeducation.com/mission.html (accessed October 5, 2013).

Fight Re[...]
Erotic E[...]

A Scree[...]
Discussi[...]
A.K. Burn[...]
Hammer, N[...]
and A.L[...]
Moderated [...]

ression of
pression

ing and
n with:
, Barbara
.M. Serra,
Steiner
y Jesse Pires

The following excerpts are taken from a panel discussion that followed a screening of short films selected by M.M. Serra. The panelists included A.K. Burns, Barbara Hammer, M.M. Serra, and A.L. Steiner. The discussion was moderated by Jesse Pires.

Jesse Pires
When I was putting together the full *Free to Love* program, I wanted to cover both mainstream films and underground films. It's implied that pornography is underground and it exists on a kind of subterranean level. That was one of the things I was thinking. This notion that mainstream is telling you what is erotic, whereas the underground is sort of asking you, "Is this erotic?" I think you can look at a lot of the stuff we saw tonight and see that there are these questions: "Is this erotic? Is the Kren film erotic?" Is it?

M.M. Serra
No.

Barbara Hammer
Who's answering that?

A.K. Burns
I think the point is not to answer the question.

Jesse Pires
Yeah, okay. That's fair.

Barbara Hammer
Maybe ask the audience.

A.K. Burns
I think that point you're making is the kind of subjective nature of sexuality. It's interesting to consider porn as a subcultural event. I think that porn actually is a mainstream event.

Jesse Pires
Well, sure, sure.

A.K. Burns
I would say that maybe we might look at commercials as a type of pornography. Do you know what I mean?

Jesse Pires

Sure.

A.K. Burns

It is interesting. I like your take on it, that it would be a statement versus a question, because I know that both Steiner and I worked out of that position when we did our film. It was very much from the question of what is possible and why do we define any of these things. You know, is that sex? Isn't it? Does it matter? No.

Jesse Pires

You view that as a kind of political gesture?

A.K. Burns

Yeah. Then something that Steiner and I always talk about is the sort of spectrum of desire which is somewhere between repulsion and attraction. I think films like *September 20* or something like that really pushed those limits of "Why wouldn't that be desire?" Of course it's desire. You're consuming and you're excreting. That's sort of, in many ways, the essence of sexuality, right?

M.M. Serra

I would say that … if you look at the beginning of the film, Kren is actually looking out a window at these gardens they have. One of the women is going to the bathroom. I think he got the idea of the eating-shitting-pissing film from watching them kind of voyeuristically and seeing what we all have in common. I'm sure he was even thinking about whether it's erotic or not. *September 20* happens to be Kren's birthday. I thought that was interesting.

In terms of pornography I always think of porn connected to the sex industry and about marketing and money rather than about personal expression. I don't use "pornography" to describe any of the films I make because I never make any money making my films. I don't make them to make money and I'm not inter-ested … because money has no intrinsic value to me. What I value is the desire to express some-thing that's deep within. Whether or not it makes money, that's not impor-tant. Actually I was asked to write, by Lynne Sachs, about a film I did called *Chop Off*. I got tired of saying, "I'm not a porn-ographer." Because my films deal with the body, but that's not marketing to make money. I said, "It's artcore," instead of hardcore, defining my work that way. Also, with a name like Mary Magdalene, the whore in the Bible, I just wanted to distance myself a little bit from it.

Barbara Hammer
You're pretty far away now. You could relax.

I want to talk about desire in terms of cinema. What turns me on is the lovely emotional breakup in Peggy Ahwesh's *Color of Love* and the great grain of black and white and the step printing of *Inter-national Darling*. I think I'm a painter at heart. My eroticism comes visually as a spectator of pieces, of works of art. They can be spray-painted or textur-ally painted or they can be these pieces that are destroyed before our eyes. I feel a connection with my body through my eyes when I watch the screen. That's sexual.

Jesse Pires
Especially in Peggy's film, the celluloid, the film itself has a kind of body, manipulated the material. That's one of the things that really resonates with me about that film as well.

A.L. Steiner
In *Razorhead* … Tom [Chomont]'s stuff is so

incredible. I always see a little bit more as the years go by. I think the idea of not being able to see something has framed some of the thinking around erotics, desire, and pleasure, and also the political body. Something about whether it's about not seeing [physically], or not seeing what's pleasurable about it at first. There's also a form of understanding desire in a different way. I think about the explicitness of commercial pornography, in which the explicit view is so important. It's almost something that reverses itself and becomes anti-erotic or sort of anti-creative in some way.

construction of gender, etc.; how it all builds on itself. For me it becomes anti-creative in the sense of sexual creativity, which is something A.K. and I were thinking about a lot with *Community Action Center*. Many of these peices tonight presented sexual creativity in explanatory ways that I hadn't previously thought about. Then I was thinking about the archive that you know about, M.M., and how much knowledge, how much information, is in Serra's head. It's kind of incredible.

M.M. Serra
You're all invited to come hang out in the archive.

Barbara Hammer
Anti-aesthetic?

A.L. Steiner
It is anti-aesthetic, but it is unaesthetic in some way to only be explicitly looking at genitalia and how genitalia feed into our

Jesse Pires
I was just going to say that I appreciate the burden that's placed on the spectator to do that work you're discussing, which is often absent in more explicit pornography. Another thing I wanted to point

out, which I mentioned when we were emailing back and forth: obviously these films are looking at ritual and poetry and fantasy. I love those terms. I think there's a lot to parse. I don't know if anyone wants to talk about ritual or poetry or fantasy. I'm introducting those terms.

Barbara Hammer
Thank you for introducing them. I'll take the challenge and …

M.M. Serra
She'll read from the book.

Barbara Hammer
Just do a little performance here, if I may.

Jesse Pires
Please.

A.K. Burns
Please.

Barbara Hammer
This is from *After Gertrude Stein*. "She was telling me, she was loving me … Every time she saw me she was telling me and telling me I didn't have to say that but wait and say whatever. Then I was waiting to tell her, waiting to be telling her, but the words kept rolling over one another coming down all unplanned … and spontaneous like fire; and she was coming over to me on the studio floor in her blindfold, and rubbing me. Then lying on me and telling me that she was. I love you so much." It goes on and on and on. I have to admit, James Broughton was my teacher.

Jesse Pires
Thank you.

A.K. Burns
What do we do after that?

A.L. Steiner
I saw *Darling International* when it premiered, at BAM [Brooklyn Academy of Music].

M.M. Serra
Oh my god, did you?

Barbara Hammer
Yeah.

M.M. Serra
That's the first time
Nicole Eisenman—

A.L. Steiner
She brought us all and
said, "I'm in this film."
She brought a date
and she brought all her
friends.

M.M. Serra
Oh my god.

A.L. Steiner
Then she said she forgot
that she had done an
explicit sex scene in it.
Then afterwards she was
sort of like—

M.M. Serra
Every time I saw her on
the street she would say
to me me, "Whatever
happened to that film you
were making?" It took
forever to get it finished

because it kept evolving
and changing.

A.K. Burns
Poetry takes a long time
to make.

A.L. Steiner
When we discussed
Multiple Orgasm together,
Barbara, you were talking
about the quietness of it
and about the politics of
that, which is also really
poetic because it's not
as if it's an explicit poem,
but there's something
about feeling other people
breathing in the room.
Just the idea of sharing
this material, which is
a sort of community-
based experience in
some way.

A.K. Burns
There's something in the
contemporary consump-
tion of pornography that
is programmed for sort
of an isolated and sham-
ing relationship to the
body, the way that the
internet has introduced

this whole other kind of isolated relationship to taking in sexual content. [Something significant] about the works that you guys made, I think, is that they required a group of people. You visited many vaginas for that piece.

Barbara Hammer
They were all my own.

M.M. Serra
They were all your own?

Barbara Hammer
Yeah, but I have many.

A.K. Burns
I think the community part extends into this, what Steiner was getting at, which is this idea that you talked about: women being in a room together and hearing each other breathe.

Barbara Hammer
Then they all held their breath.

M.M. Serra
Yeah. Do you remember that?

Barbara Hammer
That was my expectation. There would be heavy breathing but everybody was so nervous back in the '70s with this image of the convulsing vulva that nobody dared say a word.

M.M. Serra
They're still nervous now. They're still nervous and they're scared.

Barbara Hammer
Even after [Anthony] Wiener?

M.M. Serra
There's still censorship. Actually to tell you the truth, Facebook ... I wanted to put our program, the International House program on it ... The Film-Makers' Co-op is where all the films are from, but two years ago Facebook took the Film Co-op page

down because one of my students did a little ad for the Co-op going at Cooper Union with Jacob Burckhardt, and she had a weapon going, "Submit, submit your films." All of a sudden we disappeared. Facebook reprimanded us. It took two years for us to get back up. We always think the Web isn't censored, but it is, in a way. For organizations like the Film-Makers' Co-op, I'm always concerned that they'll take us down again. I noticed that the International House didn't have this, did you have this listed on…

Jesse Pires
On our Facebook page?

M.M. Serra
Yes.

Jesse Pires
Yes, I believe so.

M.M. Serra
It was on Herb [Shellenberger]'s personal Facebook page.

Jesse Pires
Right. I think we did.

A.L. Steiner
I want to start a "sit-on-my-Facebook" [page]. We would censor all non-explicit content.

Jesse Pires
Thinking about this whole series, I go back to these stories about Jack Smith's *Flaming Creatures*, screenings getting raided, police confiscating the film, which is part of underground-film lore now. There's still a considerable amount of trepidation—even with this screening. Here we are in the 21st century. I wondered, "Oh, is this okay? Is this going to be okay?"

M.M. Serra
It's still present. We're under the illusion that there's no censorship. I took a program of women's film down to the

Jacksonville Film Festival in 2006. It had *Double Your Pleasure* and *I Was A Teenage Serial Killer* by Sarah Jacobson, which was a parody of exploitation films. They put the whole audience on a bus and we went across town. We were out of the theater. They opened the Museum of Contemporary Art. I thought, "Why are we 20 minutes on a bus?" They didn't tell me till the festival was over, but the theater was owned by the Baptist Church. They didn't like the titles of the films. We were actually moved out of the theater into the Museum of Modern Art.

Barbara Hammer
That's amazing that that's happening now. I had so many of those experiences in the '70s showing my films.

M.M. Serra
Your film *Double Strength* was the first erotic film I saw by a woman which I thought really erotic. I hope you don't mind.

Barbara Hammer
I went to Buffalo. I was met by the vice squad when I was having a show at Hallwalls. This was a community affair. We're talking about community and pornography and pleasure, and I'll say erotic rather than pornography because it isn't pornographic. What did I have to do to be able to show my films? Sit there with the vice squad who are all in police uniforms and watch them. That was my audience. Talk about audience.

A.L. Steiner
Now that's pornography.

Free to

The C[…]
of the […]
Revo[…]

Film Sc[…]
Sch[…]

Love:
nema
Sexual
ution

reening
dule

Fight Repression of Erotic Expression

Program curated by M.M. Serra, followed by a public discussion with A.K. Burns, Barbara Hammer, M.M. Serra and A.L. Steiner, moderated by Jesse Pires

Wednesday, July 31, 2013, 7pm

Kurt Kren
September 20, 1967, 7 min.

James Brougton
Song of the Godbody, 1977, 11 min.

Tom Chomont
Razor Head, 1984, 4 min.

Peggy Ahwesh
The Color of Love, 1994, 10 min.

Jennifer Reeves
M.M. Serra
Darling International, 1999, 22 min.

James Franco
The Feast of Stephen, 2009, 4 min.

Friday, January 10, 2014, 7pm

Vilgot Sjöman
I am Curious (Yellow), 1967, 121 min.

Valie Export
Touch Cinema, 1968, 1 min.

Saturday, January 11, 5pm

James Bidgood
Pink Narcissus, 1971, 71 min.

Tom Chomont
Jabbok, 1967, 3 min.
Oblivion, 1969, 6 min.

Saturday, January 11, 7pm

Nagisa Oshima
In the Realm of the Senses, 1976, 109 min.

Saturday, January 11, 10pm

Gerard Damiano

Deep Throat, 1972, 61 min.

Curt McDowell

Confessions, 1972, 16 min.

Introduced by Karl McCool of Dirty Looks NYC

Thursday, January 16, 7pm

Shorts Program
Introduced by M.M. Serra

Jack Smith

Flaming Creatures, 1963, 45 min.

Carolee Schneemann

Fuses, 1967, 30 min.

Scott Bartlett

Lovemaking, 1970, 13 min.

Gunvor Nelson

Schmeerguntz, 1965, 15 min.

Kurt Kren

6/64 Mama & Papa: An Otto Muehl Happening, 1964, 4 min.

Friday, January 17, 7pm

Phyllis & Eberhardt Kronhausen

Freedom to Love, 1969, 90 min.
Introduced by Eric Schaefer

Saturday, January 18, 5pm

Knud Leif Thomsen

Gift (aka Venom), 1966, 96 min.

Saturday, January 18, 8pm

Nelson Lyon
The Telephone Book, 1971, 81 min.

Lisa Crafts
Desire Pie, 1976, 5 min.

Saturday, January 18, 10pm

Ralph Bakshi
Fritz the Cat, 1972, 78 min.

Thursday, January 23, 7pm

Frank Brittain
The Set, 1970, 102 min.

Courtesy of the National Film
and Sound Archive, Australia

Friday, January 24, 7pm

Radley Metzger

<u>Score</u>, 1972, 95 min.

Introduced by Elena Gorfinkel, followed by a discussion with director Radley Metzger

Saturday, January 25, 5pm

Jim McBride

<u>Hot Times (aka My Erotic Fantasies)</u>, 1974, 80 min.

Saturday, January 25, 7pm

Andy Warhol

<u>I, A Man</u>, 1967, 97 min.

<u>Mario Banana No. 2</u>, 1964, 3 min.

Saturday, January 25, 9pm

Paul Mazursky

Bob & Carol & Ted & Alice, 1969, 105 min.

Thursday, January 30, 7pm

Multi-Media Resource Center Program

Dirk Kortz, A Quickie, 1970, 3 min.

Laird Sutton, Rich and Judy, 1970, 12 min.

Alice Anne Parker, Riverbody, 1970, 7 min.

Constance Beeson, Holding, 1971, 13 min.

Greg Von Buchau, Love Toad, 1970, 2 min.

Laird Sutton, Fullness, 1974, 13 min.

Mariko Tse, First Date, 1976, 5 min.

Jerry Abrams, Eyetoon, 1968, 7 min.

Constance Beeson, Unfolding, 1969, 16 min.

Karen Johnson, Orange, 1971, 3 min.

Friday, January 31 at 7pm

Pat Rocco Program

A Special Friend, 1967, 15 min.

A Matter of Life, 1968, 14 min.

Sex and the Single Gay (trailer), 1970, 4 min.

Breath of Love, 1969, 20 min.

How to Shoot a Nude on the Freeway, 1969, 4 min.

Sign of Protest, 1970, 20 min.

Yes, 1968, 23 min.

Discovery, 1969, 12 min.

Introduced by Whitney Strub

Saturday, February 1, 5pm

Roger Vadim

Barbarella, 1968, 98 min.

Saturday, February 1, 7pm

Robert Downey, Sr.

No More Excuses, 1968, 46 min.

Arthur Ginsberg &
Video Free America

The Continuing Story of Carel & Ferd,
1970–75, 58 min.

Saturday, February 1, 10pm

Wakefield Poole

<u>Boys in the Sand</u>, 1971, 72 min.

Tom Chomont

<u>Love Objects</u>, 1971, 11 min.

Saturday, February 8, 5pm

Rosa von Praunheim

It is Not the Homosexual Who is Perverse,
But the Society in Which he Lives,
1971, 67 min.
Courtesy of the Reserve Film and
Video Collection of The New York
Public Library for the Performing Arts.

Southeastern Pictures Corporation

Queens at Heart, 1967, 22 min.

Saturday, February 8, 7pm

Dušan Makavejev

WR: Mysteries of the Organism, 1971, 84 min.
Introduced by J. Hoberman

Thursday, February 13, 7pm

Barbara Hammer
Early Short Films

A Gay Day, 1973, 3 min.

Menses, 1974, 4 min.

Dyketactics × 2, 1974, 8 min.

Women I Love, 1976, 27 min.

Multiple Orgasm, 1977, 10 min.

Double Strength, 1978, 15 min.

No No Nooky TV, 1987, 10 min.

Introduced by Barbara Hammer

Friday, February 14 at 7pm

Woody Allen

Everything You Always Wanted to Know About Sex* But Were Afraid to Ask, 1972, 88 min.

James Broughton

The Bed, 1968, 20 min.

Saturday, February 15, 8pm

Vilgot Sjöman

I am Curious (Blue), 1967, 107 min.

Contributors

A.K. Burns

A.K. Burns is a visual artist, performance artist, lecturer, and writer living and working in Brooklyn. She is a founding member of the activist artist group W.A.G.E. (Working Artists and the Greater Economy), and since 2010 has been the coeditor of *RANDY*, an annual trans-feminist arts magazine. In 2011 she released the feature-length video *Community Action Center* in collaboration with A.L. Steiner.

Elena Gorfinkel

Elena Gorfinkel is Assistant Professor of Art History and Film Studies at the University of Wisconsin-Milwaukee and co-editor, with John David Rhodes, of *Taking Place: Location and the Moving Image* (University of Minnesota Press, 2011.) She is currently writing a book on sexploitation cinema and film culture of the 1960s, and is editing a collection on world cinema.

Barbara Hammer

Barbara Hammer is a visual artist primarily working in film and video. She had retrospectives at the Tate Modern and Jeu de Paume in 2012, and the Museum of Modern Art, New York, in 2011. *Fearless Frames: The Films of Barbara Hammer at The Tate Modern* (Mousse Publishing, Milan) will be published in 2014.

J. Hoberman

Hoberman is Gelb Professor of Humanities at The Cooper Union in New York City. His most recent book, *Film After Film: What Was 21st Century Cinema?* (Verso, 2012), marks his eleventh book-length contribution to the fields of film and visual analysis.

Jesse Pires

Jesse Pires is Program Curator at International House Philadelphia. He co-curated the program *Pop Cinema: Art + Film in the US and UK* (2011) and *Mixed Messages: Marshall McLuhan and the Moving Image* (2012), both presented at International House. He has curated programs for the Institute of Contemporary Art, Philadelphia; Slought Foundation; and Union Docs in Brooklyn.

Eric Schaefer

Eric Schaefer is Associate Professor and Associate Chair, Department of Visual and Media Arts, Emerson College. His most recent essays appear in *The Wiley-Blackwell History of American Film* (Blackwell) and *Learning with the Lights Off: Educational Film in the United States* (Oxford University Press). His edited collection *Sex Scene: Media and the Sexual Revolution* will be published by Duke in 2014.

Contributors

Herb Shellenberger

Herb Shellenberger is a curator and filmmaker based in Philadelphia. He has curated and presented film and video programs at Vox Populi, Molodist International Film Festival (Kiev, Ukraine), and International House Philadelphia, where he has worked since 2008. He organized *The Cinema is Jonas Mekas*, a series for International House, in 2012-13.

M.M. Serra

M.M. Serra is an experimental filmmaker, curator, author, and Executive Director of Film-Makers' Cooperative. She teaches in the Media Studies program at the New School for Social Research. Anthology Film Archives presented a retrospective of her work in 2012. Her most recent films are *Breathe Deep* (2012) and *Bitch-Beauty*, which premiered at the New York Film Festival in 2011.

A.L. Steiner

A.L. Steiner is a collective member of Chicks on Speed, co-curator of *Ridykeulous*, co-founder/organizer of Working Artists and the Greater Economy (W.A.G.E.), and a collaborator with numerous visual and performing artists. Steiner was visiting faculty at Roski School of Fine Arts, University of Southern California, and 2012 Distinguished Visiting Artist at Otis College of Art & Design, Los Angeles.

Whitney Strub

Whitney Strub is an Assistant Professor of History and affiliated faculty member in the American Studies and Women's & Gender Studies programs, Rutgers University, Newark. His second book, *Obscenity Rules: Roth v. United States and the Long Struggle over Sexual Expression*, was published by the University Press of Kansas in 2013.

Colophon

Published in conjunction with the film program *Free to Love: The Cinema of the Sexual Revolution*. Organized by International House Philadelphia. Presented January 10–February 15, 2014.

Copyright © 2014 by International House Philadelphia

Texts © The authors

All rights reserved. No part of this publication may be reproduced without prior permission from the publisher.

Editors: Sheryl Conkelton & Joseph Newland, QED

Design: Mark Owens & Tanya Rubbak

Printing: The Sheridan Press

Typset in Times New Roman and ITC Franklin Gothic

DVD Design: Greenhouse Media

DVD Contents:
Desire Pie (Lisa Crafts, 1976)
A Quickie (Dirk Kortz, 1970)
Norien Ten (John Knoop, 1972)

ISBN: 978-0-615-93452-5

International House
Philadelphia
3701 Chestnut St.
Philadelphia, PA 19104
ihousephilly.org

International House Philadelphia is a multicultural residential center, a source of distinctive programming, and the embodiment of an ideal. It has a critical three-fold mission: to maintain a diverse and welcoming community for scholars from around the world, while introducing them to the American experience; to broaden the horizons of its residents and the Greater Philadelphia community through high quality international arts and humanities programs; and to encourage understanding, respect, and cooperation among the people of all nations.

Free to Love has been supported by the Pew Center for Arts & Heritage.

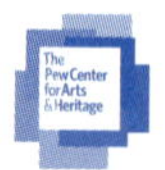
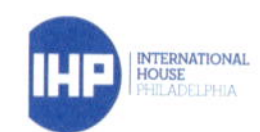